HAYNES EXTREME

ICe

The definitive guide to in-car entertainment

Haynes

Haynes Publishing

D0310974

Acknowledgements

We are grateful for the help and cooperation of numerous people in the production of this book:

Manville Smith (JL Audio)

Kimon Bellas & Damon Waters (ORCA Design & Manufacturing Corp./Focal
America, Inc.)

Robert Montenegro (SAVV Mobile Multimedia)

Jaime Palafox and Hector Galvan at SSP (Street Sound Plus), Thousand Oaks,
for help with the mobile entertainment installations

Lucette Nicoll (Nicoll Public Relations - JL Audio & SAVV)

Sue Greaves (Mitek Corporation)

Gordon Sell Public Relations (Blaupunkt North America)

Brian Shaffer (Roher Public Relations - Kenwood U.S.A.)

Kevin McDonald (Hot Import Nights - Vision Events)

Paul DiComo (Polk Audio)

Paul Sonoda (Dynamic Control - Dynamat)

Paul Papadeas (International Auto Sound Challenge Assn. - IASCA)

Gallery photos by Paul Veldboom (MEIsearch.com)

We are grateful for the help and cooperation of Mobile Electronics Certified Professionals (MECP) (owned and managed by the Consumer Electronics Association) for their help with research and providing certain portions of the material in this book.

First published 2005
Reprinted 2007

ISBN 10: 1 84425 368 6
ISBN 13: 978 1 84425 368 5

Printed by **J H Haynes & Co Ltd,**
Sparkford, Yeovil, Somerset BA22 7JJ, England.

Tel: 01963 442030 Fax: 01963 440001
Int. tel: +44 1963 442030 Fax: +44 1963 440001
E-mail: sales@haynes.co.uk
Website: www.haynes.co.uk

Haynes North America, Inc
861 Lawrence Drive, Newbury Park, California 91320, USA

Haynes Publishing Nordiska AB
Box 1504, 751 45 UPPSALA, Sweden

(H836-180-4AL1)

Be **careful** and know the **law**!

1 Advice on safety procedures and precautions is contained throughout this manual, and more specifically within the Safety section towards the back of this book. You are strongly recommended to note these comments, and to pay close attention to any instructions that may be given by the parts supplier.

2 Haynes recommends that vehicle modification should only be undertaken by individuals with experience of vehicle mechanics; if you are unsure as to how to go about the modification, advice should be sought from a competent and experienced individual. Any questions regarding modification should be addressed to the product manufacturer concerned, and not to Haynes, nor the vehicle manufacturer.

3 The instructions in this manual are followed at the risk of the reader who remains fully and solely responsible for the safety, roadworthiness and legality of his/her vehicle. Thus Haynes is giving only non-specific advice in this respect.

4 When modifying a car it is important to bear in mind the legal responsibilities placed on the owners, drivers and modifiers of cars. If you or others modify the car you drive, you and they can be held legally liable for damages or injuries that may occur as a result of the modifications.

5 The safety of any alteration and its compliance with construction and use regulations should be checked before a modified vehicle is sold as it may be an offence to sell a vehicle which is not roadworthy.

6 Any advice provided is correct to the best of our knowledge at the time of publication, but the reader should pay particular attention to any changes of specification to the vehicles, or parts, which can occur without notice.

7 Alterations to a vehicle should be disclosed to insurers and licensing authorities, and legal advice taken from the police, vehicle testing centres, or appropriate regulatory bodies.

8 Various makes of vehicle are shown being modified. Some of the procedures shown will vary from make to make; not all procedures are applicable to all makes. Readers should not assume that the vehicle manufacturers have given their approval to the modifications.

9 Neither Haynes nor the manufacturers give any warranty as to the safety of a vehicle after alterations, such as those contained in this book, have been made. Haynes will not accept liability for any economic loss, damage to property or death and personal injury other than in respect to injury or death resulting directly from Haynes' negligence.

Contents

Introduction

Head units

Speakers

01

02

03

07

08

09

Mobile Video

Navigation systems

Accessories and necessities

Subwoofers

Amplifiers

CD Changers and Digital Music Players

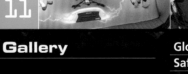

Security

Gallery

01

Introduction

Not too long ago, the average in-car entertainment system consisted of an F.M./A.M. radio and a single speaker. Not anymore.

In the last few decades, more of the comforts of home are finding their way into the car. Don't expect to see an in-dash toaster anytime soon, but CD changers, MP3 players, video systems, surround sound systems and security systems have made it possible to turn your vehicle into your "home away from home."

Even some of the components that were once hidden away by installers, such as amplifiers and subwoofers (subs), are now proudly mounted where they can be displayed. Part of the attraction is showing off this new equipment and the "installation handiwork" that went into it.

Fitting these various devices has also become easier due to the myriad installation kits now available, which has eliminated much of the custom fabrication that was once necessary. Most novices are able to install mobile electronic equipment on their own with a minimum of special tools. When carried out carefully and methodically, a professional-looking installation can be had by just about anyone with the required spare time on his or her hands.

So why bother upgrading your in-car entertainment? Because you spend a lot of time in your car - why not make it as pleasurable as possible. For most people, the daily commute represents about 1/2 hour each way. That's over 200 hours a year! And we're not counting weekend trips and holidays. So go ahead and add that amp and sub. That DVD player too; you deserve it!

But do yourself a favour before you start spending some serious coinage. Start by planning on exactly what you want from your system. Whether you're integrating with factory equipment or installing or replacing individual components, plan ahead carefully, do what you can do realistically, and don't break the bank!

Of course, not everyone will want all of the stuff described in this manual in their vehicle, and that's fine. Some will, and that's OK too, but it doesn't have to be done all at once.

Oh - with the addition of all this expensive stuff in your car or truck, you'll probably want to think seriously about a security system . . .

Connections

Throughout this manual, we will be asking you to connect wires when installing various components. In other parts of the book, in particular the "Accessories and necessities" Chapter, we will discuss the various connection types, discussing when and why they are used in your installations. Here we'd like to give you the basics on making these connections. In general, soldering makes the best connection, and the connection is corrosion resistant when done correctly, so always solder connections used in areas that could be exposed to weather. Crimp and snap-splice (Scotchlok) connections are generally used inside the vehicle. These easy-to-make connections are sometimes the only option in areas (such as deep under the dash) where soldering is impractical.

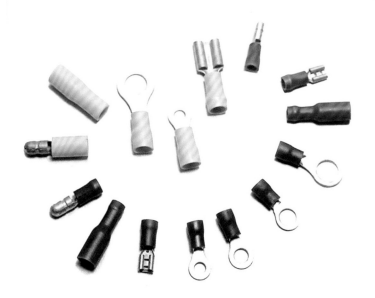

With your wires identified, how to tap into them? Before we even get that far, is that wire you're planning on playing with live?

Switch off the ignition at least - and ideally disconnect the battery before you do anything else. On cars with airbags, don't go tapping into any of the airbag wiring, which is usually bright yellow. With that cleared up, how were you planning on joining the old and new wires together?

The best options are:

Soldering - avoids cutting through your chosen wire - strip away a short section of insulation, wrap your new wire around the bared section, then apply solder to secure it. If you're a bit new to soldering, practice on a few offcuts of wire first - it ain't rocket science! Re-insulate the soldered connection afterwards, with tape or heatshrink tube.

Bullet connectors - cut and strip the end of your chosen wire, wrap your new one to it, push both into one half of the bullet. Connect the other end of your victim wire to the other bullet, and connect together. Always use the "female" half on any live feed - it'll be safer if you disconnect it than a male bullet, which could touch bare metal and send your motor up in smoke.

Block connectors - so easy to use. Just remember that the wires can come adrift if the screws aren't really tight, and don't get too ambitious about how many wires you can stuff in one hole (block connectors, like bullets, are available in several sizes). Steer clear of connectors like the one below - they're convenient, but they can give rise to problems.

With any of these options, always insulate around your connection - especially when soldering, or you'll be leaving bare metal exposed. Remember that you'll probably be shoving all the wires up into the dark recesses of the under-dash area - by the time the wires are nice and kinked/squashed together, that tiny bit of protruding wire might just touch that bit of metal bodywork, and that'll be a fire…

Head units

To give your audio system a decent start, you need a good head unit to provide the signal that an amp will beef up, and that the speakers will replay. Being the first link in the audio system's chain-of-command, makes it important to select the right head unit. You'd be well advised to spend some time selecting the right head unit for the job.

Some factory head units require removal keys. Check the Haynes manual for your vehicle for the correct removal procedure

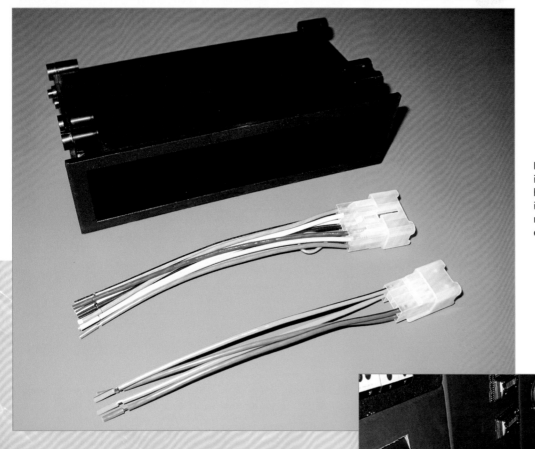

If the opening in the dash is larger than your new head unit, a vehicle-specific installation kit will be necessary to take up the extra space

Head units are usually mounted somewhere in the dash.

Today's head units are more than just volume, balance and tuning controls. Every year the manufacturers offer more exciting and high-tech features that can sometimes get confusing at the time of purchase. Take time to decide what features best suit your needs.

To avoid cutting off the factory plugs from your wiring harness, use an adapter wiring harness when installing an aftermarket radio. This enables your aftermarket radio to directly plug into your vehicle's factory harness

A few things to think about:

CD Changer Controls: Does the head unit have the ability to control an external CD changer? Most aftermarket head units are designed only to work with changers of the same brand, although adapters are available which enable a head unit with changer controls to function with a different brand changer.

Satellite Radio Controls: This type of head unit can accommodate the separate satellite tuner module connections and has built-in controls for tuning the stations.

Preamp Outputs: Output jacks located on the back of the unit that supply signal to a separate amplifier via RCA leads.

Changer Direct Digital: A connection from the head unit to the changer that can be a special multi-pin cable, fibre optics, or digital coax cable.

In-dash Hard Drives: A type of head unit that has the ability to store hours of digital music files that have been downloaded from your computer.

CD-R, CD-RW/Digital Playback Capability: Are you going to play CD's you've ripped with MP3s? If fitting hours of music onto one disc is your thing, you'll need to purchase a head unit compatible with CD-R or CD-RW discs.

ID3 Tags: Is the head unit going to play MP3 tracks? If so, consider purchasing a unit that displays the identity of each track.

Displays: Audio head units are available with a variety of different types of displays; multi-color backlighting, dot matrix text, touch screen programming, multi-color animated LCDs, and even screensavers you can customize with your own photos or text messages.

Theft Deterrence: While no theft system for your head unit is completely foolproof, several manufacturers have developed different strategies for the battle against car stereo thieves. A common type of theft-prevention design is the detachable face. This feature enables the owner to remove the control panel from the unit and carry it in a pocket or purse. Another type of security would be the hidden face design. The control panel and display go black when the unit is turned off; when the stereo is turned off the thief is fooled into thinking the head unit is just a black panel on the dash board. Other manufacturers have designed a similar idea, having the control panel retract when the power is turned off, leaving a black panel concealing any controls or display.

Remote control: A wireless remote control that usually adjusts volume and preset scans. A handy feature to help keep your eyes on the road while driving.

01 First, the old set's got to be shifted. Resist the urge to just crowbar the thing out of the dash - you'll be needing two of the standard radio removal tools to do the job with less damage. And you could always sell it, or keep it, to stick back in when you sell the car?

Installation

05 . . . and secure it by bending over just a few of the triangular lugs (not all of them!).

02 Another reason not to get too excited when removing the old set is that most of the wiring behind is fully 'recyclable' - ie we'll be using it again. One bonus on our car - it's got ISO plugs for power and speakers, meaning our new set should plug straight in.

03 The old cage has to go too - you can't use this with your new set, or the locking pins won't engage. Most DIY-fitted cages have absolutely every last locking tab bent over, which makes it a long job with a small screwdriver to remove it.

⚠ Warning: *If you're working on an airbag-equipped vehicle, see the Warning on page 71 before starting this procedure.*

04 With the old cage out of the picture, now's a good time to introduce the new set's cage into the equation . . .

Having ISO plugs makes life much easier - one does power, the other speakers (the power one has red, yellow and black leads, among others). Here, we're plugging in the original speaker wiring plug to the new headset wiring . . .

. . . and now, we're cutting the original speaker wires. Why? We're going to run rear 6x9s off the headset, so . . .

. . . we'll be joining on some decent speaker wire to run to the back of the car. By using the new headset's wiring instructions (these tell you which colour wires are front/rear, positive/negative), when you connect the original speaker plug, you can work out which of the original speaker wires did what.

09 Any original speaker wires you're not using should be chopped and taped-up. If you're running all your new speakers amped, just leave the original ISO speaker plug disconnected.

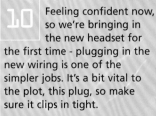

10 Feeling confident now, so we're bringing in the new headset for the first time - plugging in the new wiring is one of the simpler jobs. It's a bit vital to the plot, this plug, so make sure it clips in tight.

11 Power to the headset comes straight from the old ISO wiring plug (this provides permanent and ignition lives, and an earth). Plug this into your headset wiring socket, and it's hot (so leave the ignition key off for now).

12 Virtually all headsets provide an output for remotely switching-on your amps (or for powering-up an electric aerial). Called the 'remote' or 'P-cont' wire, it's usually blue, and should be joined to your own wire which will run back to the amps. One of our RCA leads has a built-in P-cont, so we'd be pretty stupid not to use it.

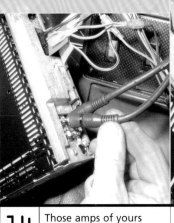

13 When you're confronted with a mass of wiring you can't sort out, don't forget the manual. Our man's got the right idea. Well, it's a lot better than blowing up your headset.

14 Those amps of yours need a signal to work from, and that's what the RCA outputs on the headset provide. If your set's got more than one pair of connections (pre-outs), these may be marked 'front', 'rear' or 'sub'. Use whichever set makes sense for your system. Connect the plug with the red stripe to the red socket - we think you can guess where the other one goes.

15 Don't forget to plug in the aerial lead if you plan on listening to Hip-Hop FM. Grrrreat. If the lead won't fit, you might need an adapter plug. Or you might find (like us) that an adapter plug's been fitted to your lead - all you need do then is take it off.

16 Test that everything's working at this point, before pushing the unit right into its cage. If all's well, push the headset home until it clicks. If it gets stuck, take the set out, and un-bunch all the wiring by hand. Do not force it in, or you could end up having a very bad day. If you have trouble, unclipping the carpet from the front of the centre console gets you in behind. Success? Now get out the instruction manual again, and set those levels properly. Enjoy.

An installation kit

This factory Double DIN head unit is replaced . . .

. . . with the help of an installation kit . . .

. . . with an aftermarket DIN head unit.

Not long ago, the car stereo industry accepted the DIN (7 1/8" x 2") as the standard head unit chassis size. This enabled aftermarket companies to manufacture installation kits for many different makes of cars. Major dash surgery was no longer necessary when installing an aftermarket head unit.

Head Units

If my current factory head unit is Double DIN, can I replace it with a DIN size aftermarket head unit?

Yes, depending on the availability of an aftermarket installation kit for your particular vehicle model.

What is an adapter harness?

This is a wiring harness that allows you to disconnect your standard radio and connect an aftermarket head unit without cutting your factory wiring.

What is the AUX input jack used for on the front of my head unit?

This is for connecting an additional source to the head unit, maybe a portable CD or MP3 player.

My head unit can identify ID-3 tags. What is an ID-3 tag?

An ID-3 tag is the displayed information identifying each audio track on a text-encoded MP3 disc,

What are the RCA outputs used for on the back of my head unit?

These are usually low-level signal outputs for connecting an external amplifier.

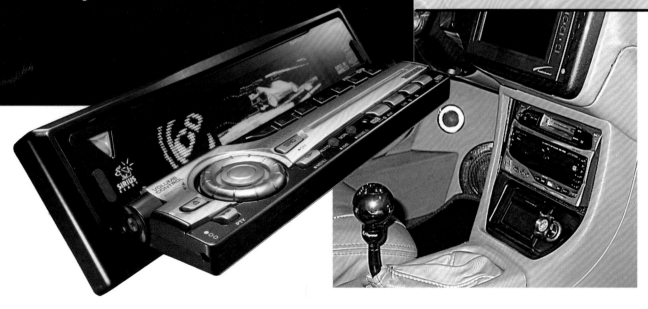

Speakers

The most important components in your sound system are the speakers. Sure, the source unit from where the speakers receive their signal is also very important, but it's up to the speakers to actually convert that signal into the sound that you hear. (Keep in mind, though, if your head unit is putting out a poor signal, a good speaker will do its best to reproduce that bad signal, with the results you might expect!)

The speaker can represent the easiest way to upgrade an existing system or the final step in an expensive custom sound system. That's why it's important to understand what a speaker does and how it works. Let's take a look at the components that make up a typical speaker.

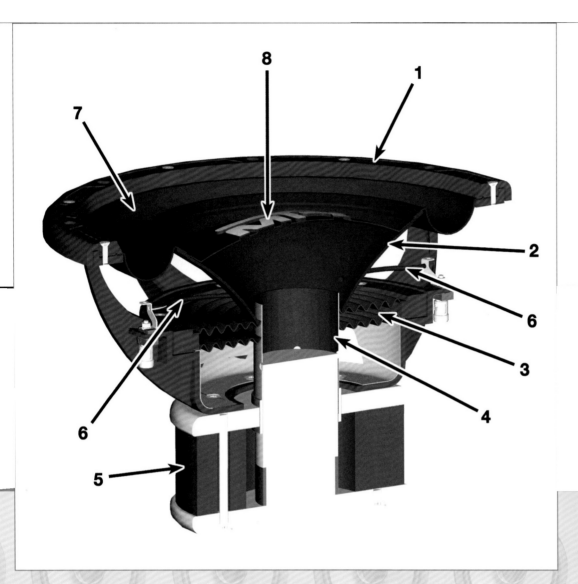

1 Frame

The frame provides a solid support (most are stamped steel) for the components and holds them in alignment.

2 Diaphragm (or cone)

The diaphragm is usually made of treated paper or polypropylene and is connected to the voice coil. The diaphragm vibrates to send the movement of the voice coil out into the air as sound waves.

3 Spider

Made of special treated cloth, the flexible round ribbed spider provides support for the diaphragm by filling the space between it and the frame.

4 Voice coil

The voice coil is made up of wire wound around a tube called a former that moves in and out within the assembly between the core and the magnet, kind of like a piston.

5 Magnet

The magnet provides a magnetic field for the voice coil to react against.

6 Tensile leads

These thin, flexible leads carry the amplifier's electrical signal from the speaker terminals to the voice coil.

7 Surround

The diaphragm's outer circumference attaches to the frame by the flexible surround. The surround controls the diaphragm's movement so it maintains its shape as it moves in and out. These are usually constructed from foam or rubber.

8 Dust cap

As its name implies, the dust cap is a dome located in the centre of the diaphragm that keeps dust out of the voice coil. It also helps to project sound.

One set of each of these components makes up a speaker "driver." Drivers that handle the highest frequencies are *tweeters* and are generally quite small. Drivers that handle the lower frequencies are called *woofers* and are much bigger. Drivers that handle the frequencies in between are, appropriately named, *mid-range drivers*. Drivers that handle the ultra-low frequencies are called *subwoofers or subs* and can be quite large and ridiculously heavy (see the next chapter for more information on subwoofers).

A speaker with only one driver is known as a *one-way* speaker. A speaker with two drivers, for example a mid-range and a tweeter, is called a *two-way or coaxial* speaker. If it combines a woofer, mid-range and tweeter, it's a *three-way or triaxial* speaker.

The reason for having these different size drivers is simple; to project as accurately as possible the sound that the signal from the head unit is trying to reproduce. A large driver would fail miserably trying to create a high-frequency sound, simply because it can't vibrate fast enough. A tweeter couldn't possibly produce a bass note because of its short travel and inability to move the required amount of air. But all combined, an accurate reproduction of the sound being transmitted or played on the head unit can be achieved. In order for this to happen, however, the frequencies have to be divided up and sent to the proper drivers. This is done by a special filter called a crossover, which will be explained later.

Shopping for speakers

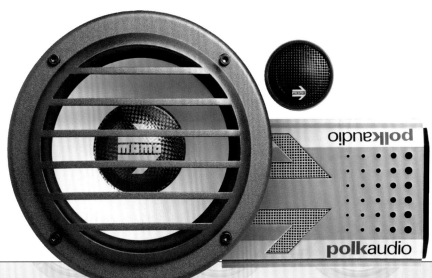

So you want higher-fidelity sound from your system and you've decided to change out your speakers. Now what?

First you have to decide if you're just going to swap your factory speakers for higher-quality units that will drop right into place without any modifications, or go with component speakers that will require some fabrication to accommodate them.

Let's say you want to buy speakers that will fit perfectly in the standard locations. Here are a few things you'll want to toss around in your mind:

- **Size** - Diameter, depth and, on coaxial, triaxial and quadaxial speakers, tweeter protrusion. You have to make sure that the locations in which the replacement speakers will be mounted will accept the speakers. Many retailers will have specifications for your exact vehicle, along with a list of speakers you can choose from.

- **Continuous power rating** - This spec, measured in watts RMS, is the amount of power the speaker needs to operate at a sensible level.

- **Peak power handling capability** - This rating indicates the speaker's "redline," measured in watts. It's the amount of power the speaker can handle in short bursts, not sustained levels.

- **Efficiency (or sensitivity)** - This rating indicates the speaker's ability to put out sound with a certain power input. A speaker with a higher efficiency or sensitivity rating will be louder than a speaker with a lower rating given the same input power. Pick speakers with a high efficiency rating if you have a relatively low-powered standard head unit. If you're running an external amp or have a high-powered head unit, low efficiency speakers are OK (they just require more power to drive them).

- **Price** - As with most anything, you get what you pay for when you buy speakers. Generally the most expensive speakers you can afford will give you the best performance.

You may also want to consider installing coaxial, triaxial or quadaxial speakers (also known as two-way, three-way and four-way speakers). This will give you a broader range of sound coming from the speaker mounting location. Some experts recommend going with coaxials; they say the higher ranges get a little harsh with the triaxials and quadaxials. The only way to really tell if a speaker suits your tastes, though, is to "audition" it for yourself. Most good stereo shops are equipped to let you do this, and even though it won't sound exactly the same as it would in your vehicle, it'll give you a good idea of its sound characteristics.

How a speaker works

The system amplifier (whether it be a separate component or built into the head unit) sends alternating negative and positive signals to the voice coil. The voice coil moves back and forth like a piston within the magnet in response to these positive and negative signals (it essentially becomes an electromagnet travelling inside the permanent magnet). The movement (vibration) of the coil turns into sound by transmitting the motion to the speaker diaphragm, which produces the air movement, causing sound waves to be projected into the air.

The faster the air moves, the higher the frequency produced. A voice coil on a lower frequency speaker such as a 50Hz woofer, for example, moves back and forth 50 times per second, while on a higher frequency speaker such as a 20kHz tweeter, the coil will move up to 20,000 times a second.

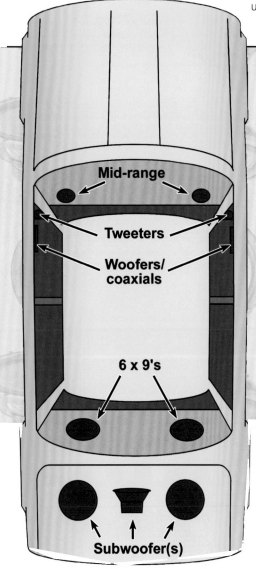

Mid-range

Tweeters

Woofers/ coaxials

6 x 9's

Subwoofer(s)

Speaker placement

How the speakers are arranged plays an important role in the "soundstage," or where the music seems to be coming from. When you listen to a live performance the musicians are in front of you, spread out across the stage. It's easier to determine the location from where the higher frequencies are emanating, a little less so for the mid-range tones (because they are usually the most prevalent), and actually difficult to tell from where the bass is originating. Try walking around a concert hall sometime and compare the differences between the tones; no matter where you go, the bass will sound pretty much the same, but the mids and highs will be noticeably different depending on where you are.

Therefore, it makes sense to use this analogy when deciding where to install aftermarket speakers. This is easier said than done, though, because you are somewhat limited in your choices of placement since you're working in a very confined space instead of a stage!

- If you're simply replacing your factory speakers with higher quality units, you obviously can't do a whole lot to alter the soundstage, but you definitely will notice an improvement in sound quality. Replacing a standard mid-range speaker with a coaxial or triaxial speaker that will

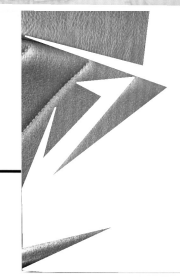

drop right into the factory mounting hole is an excellent option, and easy to do. Some of these units are equipped with tweeters that can be rotated and "aimed" to compensate for a less-than-ideal mounting location.

• If you're installing component speakers (separate tweeters, mid-range and woofers/subwoofer), you'll want to mount the tweeters up front and fairly high, aimed toward the centre of the front seats. Ideally the mid-range speakers would be mounted in the dash, pointing at the front seat occupants. Specially formed kick panels designed to aim mid-range speakers towards the occupants are also available. Woofers can be mounted down low, since it's harder to detect the source of bass anyway. Subwoofers, pumping out ultra-low frequencies, can be mounted just about anywhere there's room to fit them.

It's worth mentioning that no matter how well done any given sound system is, it won't necessarily please everyone. Just as beauty is in the eye of the beholder, sound quality (and the enjoyment it brings) is in the ear of the listener.

Kick panel speaker enclosures

Kick panels are a great place to mount speakers, but to do it properly takes quite a bit of fabrication. You don't want to just mount a speaker flush in a kick panel (even if there is enough room for it), because it would point right at the occupants' feet. Rather than cannibalise and modify your existing kick panels, you can purchase custom replacement kick panels that'll fit right into place, match your interior and fire the speakers right up at you. This will give you a decent soundstage with a minimum of effort.

Speaker polarity

When installing speakers, whether they be drop-in replacements for factory units or part of a full-on custom installation, you'll have to determine their polarity before connecting the wires to them. This is important because the signals that the speakers receive cause the voice coils and diaphragms to move inward and outward, thus producing sound. BUT, if one speaker is wired one way and the other speaker is wired just the opposite, parts of the sound spectrum could be cancelled out, or at least be affected in a bad way. That's why you need to figure out the positive and negative terminal of each speaker if it isn't clearly marked (the positive terminal will either be labeled with a + or a spot of coloured paint).

Attach a set of jumper leads to the terminals of a typical 1.5-volt battery (the size of the battery doesn't matter - it could be a D-cell or an AA). You can solder or tape the leads in place. Now touch the leads to the terminals of the speaker and watch what happens to the diaphragm (cone) of the speaker. If it moves outward, the jumper lead from the positive battery terminal is touching the positive terminal of the speaker. If the cone is pulled inward, the jumper lead from the positive battery terminal is touching the negative terminal of the speaker. Mark the speaker terminals accordingly, then make sure the positive signal wire is attached to the positive terminal at each speaker.

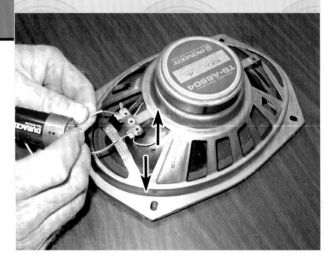

Other items you may need for speaker installation

In addition to the speakers themselves, here are some items that you should pick up before you go back home to do the install:

• **Wire** - If you are doing a custom install and mounting speakers in places other than the standard locations, make sure you have plenty of speaker wire. Once your interior is all torn apart, you don't want to be caught short of wire and have to piece it back together to drive back to the stereo shop!

• **Connectors and solder -** These are the staples of the installation. Figure out what kind of connectors you need and how many, then buy more than that. When soldering splices or connectors, use only resin core solder.

• **Shrink tubing** - Along with the connectors and solder, get some shrink tubing to cover your solder joints. It makes for a much cleaner-looking installation than electrician's tape, not to mention a more secure and longer-lasting one.

• **Jumper harnesses** - Check on the availability of special jumper harnesses that will connect your new speakers directly to your vehicle's wiring harness. These will make an easy job even quicker and easier and will allow you to retain your original electrical connectors just in case you wish to sell the car someday and reinstall the old speakers.

Crossovers

Crossovers separate different frequency bands and redirect them to the proper drivers. Without some type of crossover, these ranges of sound can't be separated, resulting in an audio system that sounds "flat" and/or distorted. So, they're incorporated into the system to send the high frequencies to the tweeters, mid-range frequencies to the mid-range speakers, low frequencies to the woofers, and ultra-low frequencies to the subwoofer(s), if used. Some are adjustable and can be set to separate these ranges at certain frequencies, thereby eliminating the frequencies that the speaker can't use (or that would cause it to operate inefficiently). Others aren't adjustable, and some are built right into a component (like a triaxial speaker).

There are two types of crossovers: active and passive. Active crossovers are placed into the signal chain before the amplifier, and require a separate DC voltage input to operate. Some amplifiers have built-in active crossovers.

Passive crossovers are placed into the signal chain between the amplifier and the speakers. They don't require DC voltage to operate. And, since they are connected just before the speakers, one amplifier can drive a number of speakers correctly.

Rear shelf & **speakers**

You can always try hacking your rear side panels about for speakers, but that means leaving them in there when you sell the car on. Speakers work best when rigidly mounted, so shelf-mounting is the simplest and best option. If you don't want to butcher your standard shelf (always a flimsy item), either make a new one from MDF, using your stock shelf as a template, or buy a ready-made acoustic shelf. Either way, make hiding your new speakers a priority - tasty speakers on display in the back window could soon mean no rear window, and no speakers...

02 With a speaker outline marked, remove the wood from the rest of the shelf, and drill a nice big hole somewhere inside it . . .

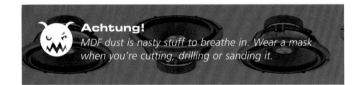

Achtung!
MDF dust is nasty stuff to breathe in. Wear a mask when you're cutting, drilling or sanding it.

03 . . . then get busy with the jigsaw.

Use the speaker mounts (or even the speakers themselves) as a template to drill the mounting holes . . . **04**

. . . then screw on the speakers themselves. Don't forget that 6x9s can be run off the headset, to provide a little "rear fill" - if you have them amped-up, you might find that the sound's too biased to the back of the car. **05**

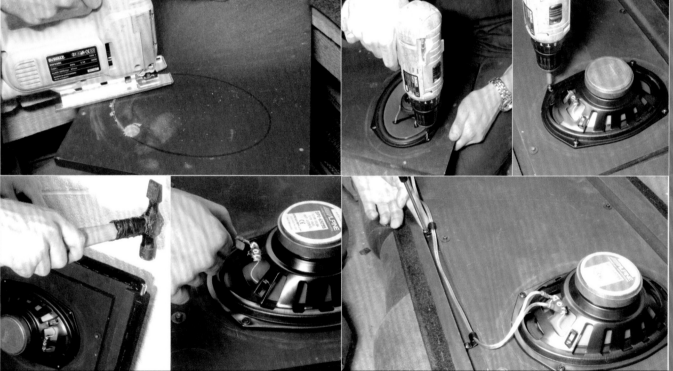

06 One useful feature of a ready-made shelf is that it comes with hinge pins, and even with pre-drilled holes to take them. A few light taps with the hammer, and the shelf's ready to fit. If you're putting a sub box in the boot as well, it's not a bad idea to plonk the box and shelf in, to check your speaker magnets will clear above the box. Just a thought...

07 Remember that the length of wire to each speaker should be the same (as near as poss), or you might find the speakers run slightly out of phase. Crimp on the right terminals, and connect up your speakers.

08 For max neatness, use P-clips screwed along the edge of the shelf. If you plan on being able to take the shelf out easily, you'll be needing a Neutrik plug and socket, which allows quick and easy wiring disconnection. Using the instructions provided with the connector, connect up your pos and neg speaker wires, and assemble the plug. Ordinary folk just fit bullet connectors at the side of the shelf, which work just as well (but don't look as flash).

Direct replacement rear speakers

01 Unclip and remove the rear side panels to get access to the rear speaker, then undo the four speaker screws . . .

02 . . . disconnect the wiring plug, and the old unit's a goner. But don't bin it, unless you're sure you'll sell the car with its ICE install intact.

03 Now for the first trial fitting of our new 6x9s. We were lucky on the front doors - they went straight in . . .

04 . . . this time, our luck ran out - the magnet wouldn't sink in far enough. Having found another use for our tin of grease (something round to mark the outline) . . .

Speakers

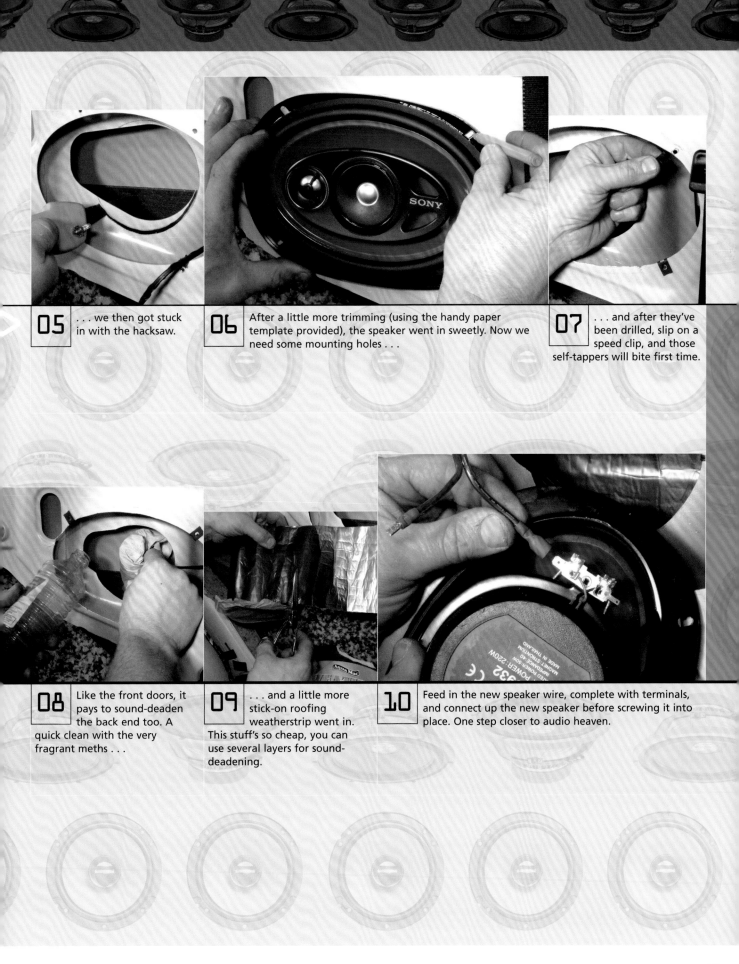

05 . . . we then got stuck in with the hacksaw.

06 After a little more trimming (using the handy paper template provided), the speaker went in sweetly. Now we need some mounting holes . . .

07 . . . and after they've been drilled, slip on a speed clip, and those self-tappers will bite first time.

08 Like the front doors, it pays to sound-deaden the back end too. A quick clean with the very fragrant meths . . .

09 . . . and a little more stick-on roofing weatherstrip went in. This stuff's so cheap, you can use several layers for sound-deadening.

10 Feed in the new speaker wire, complete with terminals, and connect up the new speaker before screwing it into place. One step closer to audio heaven.

Custom rear speakers

We didn't want to keep our old side trim panels, having made our own from alloy plate. We didn't fancy mounting a speaker on
01 tinny alloy, so we cut two strips of thick steel, mounted our speaker plate onto them, and welded the strips to the rear arch and door pillar. Just a bit extreme.

A few strips (slices?) of sound-deadening, and our
02 vibration worries from the car disappeared.

The 6x9s we chose are being run from the headset (a bit of a waste, as they're rated at 400W), so at least we're keeping something simple.
03 Attach terminals to oxygen-free speaker wiring, and connect up.

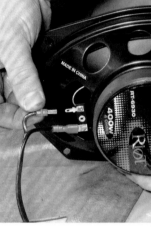

04 Oh man - these are some sexy-looking speakers. We're not covering them up too much. We mounted ours rigidly to the metal strips we fitted earlier, using longer-than-necessary bolts. Why? You'll see in a minute.

05 Speaker grilles? Who needs 'em? Certainly not the standard items, anyway. This is a section of grille mesh (the stuff you might normally find in a bumper) which we put to good use. Cut it to shape, make holes for those four over-long bolts we fitted earlier . . .

06 . . . and slide in our new side trim panel, lovingly trimmed from ally (and still wearing its plastic protective coating, which we'll peel off later). In case you're wondering, yes, we did sound-deaden the tinny new panel on the back, before fitting it.

07 Four carefully-drilled holes in the new trim panel later, and now our speaker's rigidly mounted to the car and the panel. And it shouldn't vibrate (especially with only 50W of headset power per channel through it). Yes, the 6x9s do sound lush - as good as they look, in fact.

28

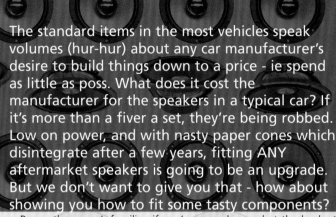

The standard items in the most vehicles speak volumes (hur-hur) about any car manufacturer's desire to build things down to a price - ie spend as little as poss. What does it cost the manufacturer for the speakers in a typical car? If it's more than a fiver a set, they're being robbed. Low on power, and with nasty paper cones which disintegrate after a few years, fitting ANY aftermarket speakers is going to be an upgrade. But we don't want to give you that - how about showing you how to fit some tasty components?

Boss - the name's familiar, if you've ever shopped at the budget end of the market. But do not be fooled - Boss make several ranges, and until now, we've only seen the very cheapest range in the UK (for more info, check the DD Audio website - www.ddaudio.co.uk). These very tasty-looking items very obviously come from their more expensive range - so let's see if the sound matches the looks...

Front
speakers

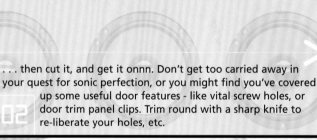

Once you've got the door trim panel off, and have removed (and burnt) the old speaker, it's time to think vibration. If you don't want all that kicking power to set your door panel tizzing, you need to invest in some sound-deadening. Yes, the market leader's **01** Dynamat - but - it comes at a price. What else is out there? Brown Bread. Sounds dead. Clean up the door panel with some decent solvent . . .

. . . then cut it, and get it onnn. Don't get too carried away in your quest for sonic perfection, or you might find you've covered up some useful door features - like vital screw holes, or **02** door trim panel clips. Trim round with a sharp knife to re-liberate your holes, etc.

>>

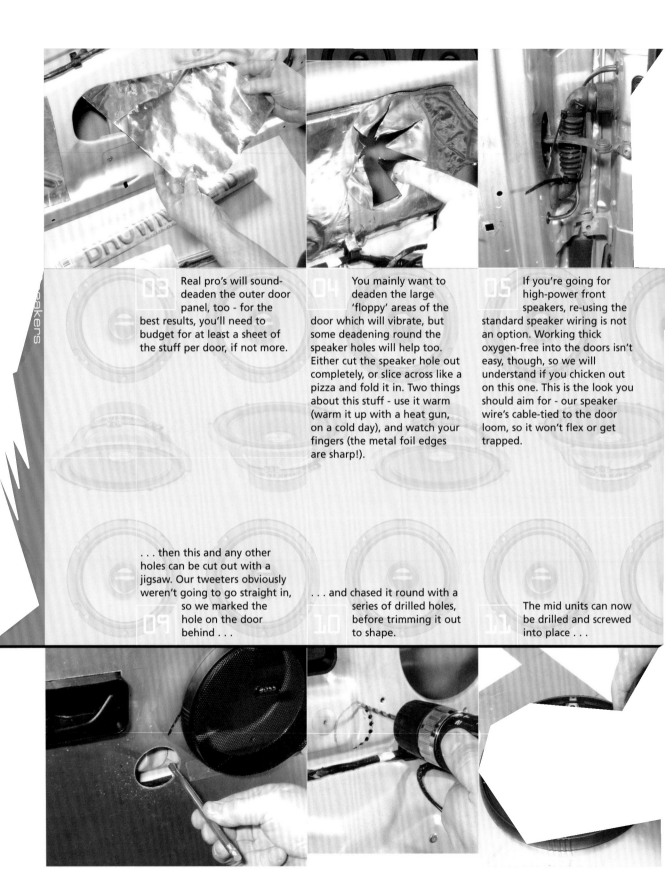

03 Real pro's will sound-deaden the outer door panel, too - for the best results, you'll need to budget for at least a sheet of the stuff per door, if not more.

04 You mainly want to deaden the large 'floppy' areas of the door which will vibrate, but some deadening round the speaker holes will help too. Either cut the speaker hole out completely, or slice across like a pizza and fold it in. Two things about this stuff - use it warm (warm it up with a heat gun, on a cold day), and watch your fingers (the metal foil edges are sharp!).

05 If you're going for high-power front speakers, re-using the standard speaker wiring is not an option. Working thick oxygen-free into the doors isn't easy, though, so we will understand if you chicken out on this one. This is the look you should aim for - our speaker wire's cable-tied to the door loom, so it won't flex or get trapped.

09 . . . then this and any other holes can be cut out with a jigsaw. Our tweeters obviously weren't going to go straight in, so we marked the hole on the door behind . . .

10 . . . and chased it round with a series of drilled holes, before trimming it out to shape.

11 The mid units can now be drilled and screwed into place . . .

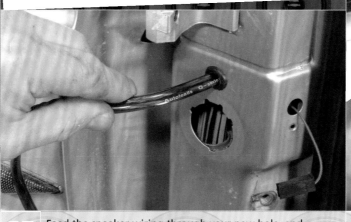
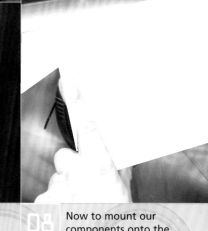

06 Drilling holes in the A-pillar for door speaker wiring is much easier with those pesky doors out of the way - and removing them isn't hard (see your trusty Haynes manual for details). While the door's off, drill a similar hole in that, below where the door loom plugs in.

07 Feed the speaker wiring through your new hole, and please use a grommet on the sharp edges. If you don't, the best that might happen is your tunes will suddenly stop. At worst, you might blow a channel on your system.

08 Now to mount our components onto the doors. Of course, our panels are a tad unusual, being home-made alloy, but the ideas are the same. Either use the mounting plate or the template provided to mark your hole, making sure the hole lines up with the one behind, in the door itself . . .

. . . while the tweeters have their own clever little mounting bracket which screws on from behind.

12

Most component sets have a separate crossover - our crossovers look like something out of Star Trek, so we couldn't just hide them under the dash. With a hole drilled (and grommeted) in our door panel to take the speaker wires, it's time to wire them up. Check your set's instructions for which speaker connects where, and where the amp feed goes in.

13

Most tweeters come pre-wired, but the mids need terminals. Make sure your speaker connections are secure - it's also worth wrapping them with tape, just in case they touch metal inside the door when the panel goes back on.

14

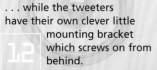

FAQs
Speakers

Courtesy of Polk Audio

Can my car stereo really hurt my ears?

Sure. Prolonged exposure to sound pressure levels of about 85dB will cause permanent hearing damage. Professional audio competitions specify the use of hearing protection devices for their contests, especially at higher volume levels. You can test the dB level of your car stereo with a Sound Pressure Level Meter. If you're disoriented and your hearing is sort of muffled after you've been listening to your car stereo, or you hear ringing in your ears, then turn it down! If you have to shout at the person in the passenger seat, and you're not angry with them, then it's a good bet that your stereo is too loud. For the sake of your hearing, turn it down.

Why did my speaker blow?

Most speakers fail due to excess distortion caused by an amplifier being pushed beyond its power capabilities. When an amplifier is driven beyond its safe operating range, it distorts or 'clips' the audio signal, and sends this clipped signal to the speaker. This produces both mechanical and thermal stresses on the voice coil. In plain English, the voice coil gets banged around and overheated and breaks. Although it doesn't make "common sense," you're less likely to blow a speaker by using too much power than not enough. If you like to play it loud, get a bigger amplifier.

The other common cause of speaker failure is trying to get too much high volume bass out of a small speaker. Eventually the speaker reaches its excursion limit, its limit of physical travel. The voice coil bangs around, gets bent and the speaker breaks. This is a common problem with the smaller full-range and coaxial speakers. There's an easy way to prevent this type of failure – limit the lowest bass frequencies to the driver with an in-line capacitor or "bass blocker." You'll only be filtering out the bass frequencies the speaker can't reproduce so you won't be missing anything, especially if you're using a subwoofer. Any car stereo installer can help you choose the right value for your speakers.

How much power would work well with my speakers?

If you read the previous FAQ, you already know that you're better off with too much power than not enough. But like everything else in life, too much of even a good thing can be bad; speakers can be overpowered.

All speakers come with power handling specs; you should use these to determine how much power you will need. There are two kinds of power handling specs: continuous (RMS) power handling, and peak or max power handling. Continuous describes the power handling with a constant volume test tone. The peak power handling describes how much power the speaker can handle on a very time-limited basis, usually on the order of milliseconds. As music is transient in nature (the volume goes up and down a lot) the peak or max rating is the most useful for determining amp size for a given pair of speakers. For example, for a speaker rated at 100 watts peak, get a 100 watts/channel amplifier to safely get the greatest amount of volume from that speaker. If all you know is the continuous rating of a speaker, use the 3/4 rule, divide the continuous rating by 0.75 to calculate the maximum amplifier size. For example, a speaker with a 50 watt continuous rating can be safely used with an amplifier of 70 watts/channel (50÷0.75 = 66.7, round up to 70 watts).

How do I tell if my speakers are in or out of phase?

If your speakers are out of phase, imaging will be vague and bass output will be reduced. To ensure that your speakers are hooked up in phase, check to make sure that the positive and negative leads are connected the same way to both your speakers and your receiver or amp. Make sure red is connected to red, black to black, etc. Check for correct phasing using a 1.5-volt battery. Disconnect the speaker wire from the amp. Touch the wire you think is negative to the negative battery terminal. Touch the positive wire to the positive battery terminal. If your speakers are wired in phase, the speaker cone will move "out" and stay there. If they are out of phase, the driver cone will move "in" and stay there. (This won't help you for tweeters, only midrange and woofers. So when you're wiring your tweeters, be careful. Do it right the first time.)

Phasing is never absolute in car audio situations, since speakers are rarely facing the same directions. Phasing differences mostly affect bass. Is your system totally lacking bass? Try changing the phase on your sub system. 90% of the time, that's the key to more bass!

How do I use my faders and balance settings to make my system sound better?

Proper setting of your front-to-rear fader and left/right balance controls is important for optimum staging and imaging in your system. Too much sound in the rear of the car (sometimes called "rear fill") will often eliminate staging altogether, forcing sound away from the front of the car, while too little rear fill will sound dull. Too much sound on one side of the car or the other will add an unrealistic element to the imaging. To adjust fade and balance, play a tape or CD you are familiar with and turn the rear speakers on full with the fade control. Listen to the rear speakers, and then slowly turn the fade up in the front speakers just until you can't tell the rear speakers are playing anymore, then ease off a tad. You're probably close to optimum setting when the front staging is such that the rear speakers provide little more than ambiance and space to the sound. Test it by going full on the front speakers (without losing the position you just attained). You'll hear an immediate loss of spaciousness in the sound with the rear speakers faded all the way down. Return to your optimum setting.
Setting the balance is more difficult, so it's always a good idea to leave the balance setting at the "12 o'clock" position. That's as close to equal as you're going to be able to hear with your own ears.

My system "pops" when I turn it off. How do I stop it?

As you power down, transient signals in the processor sometimes find their way into the signal path. The amp transmits them to the speakers, and POP! Add some "turn off delay" to your head unit. Refer to the owner's manual that came with your head unit.

Do round speakers sound better than oval speakers?

For all practical purposes, yes. A round cone is more rigid than an oval-shaped cone. At higher sound levels, an oval-shaped cone will distort more. Oval-shaped speakers are made to please the rear shelf space considerations of many cars. One advantage of 6x9s, though, is that ovals have more area, and thus move higher air volume and produce more bass.

Where should I put my tweeters for best performance?

The best thing to do is to install the rest of the system and leave the wires for the tweeters long. Grab a buddy (you've got one, right?) and have them hold one tweeter while you hold the other. (This helps you get them separated by the width of the car, something you'll find very hard to do by yourself.) Play some music that you're familiar with and put the tweeter in different locations with your buddy mirroring your placement. Listen for "staging" and "imaging." When you find a spot that works well, mount them there, if you can. If you can't put them where they sound the best, compromise by mounting them on the front door frame (inside, opposite the side view mirror) facing the space between the two front seats.

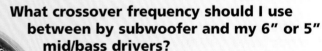

When I turn my music up, my headlights dim. How come?

Your headlights dim because your system has caused a drop in the available voltage for your car's other, less necessary accessories (headlights, engine, etc.). Voltage drops can be caused by an accessory's large current demand, like an amp struggling to produce a loud bass note. Get your battery and alternator checked. A low battery can overload an alternator, drawing power away from your system. If everything checks out okay, you could be making such large demands on your electrical system that an upgraded alternator may be necessary. A "stiffening" capacitor can also be installed. A stiffening capacitor is like an extra power supply for your electrical system; it keeps a small reserve of 12-volt power. If your car won't start after you play the stereo for a long time with the engine off, try paralleling another battery into your system.

What crossover frequency should I use between by subwoofer and my 6" or 5" mid/bass drivers?

There's no quick and easy answer to this question. It depends on the car and the total design of the system. Generally you don't want a subwoofer to go much higher than 100Hz and 200Hz is the absolute limit. Typically when you set your subwoofer crossover point you will use that as a starting point for your high-pass on your mid/bass drivers. Sometimes you will need to increase the crossover frequency and sometimes you will need to lower it. It is basically all a matter of personal preference and the acoustics of your car. Electronic crossovers make it very easy to try a variety of crossover frequencies to see what works best for you and your car.

Should I use an electronic (active) crossover or a passive crossover?

Electronic crossovers are better and allow greater ease of system tuning, but require the use of more amplifiers and thus expense. Passive crossovers are the way to go if your don't have the money for the additional amplifiers. Be careful with using electronic crossovers for tweeter high-pass filters. Setting a tweeter's crossover point too low may blow the tweeter.

What brand of amplifiers do you recommend?

We recommend that you stick with well-known brands that are available. Most car audio retailers can help with this selection. Beware of "bargain" amps; too much power for too little money generally means that corners have been cut somewhere in quality of construction or service support.

How loud will my speakers play?

Look up the sensitivity rating of the speaker, which is expressed in dB/watt/metre. For example a speaker with an 89dB sensitivity will produce 89dB of sound 1 metre (39") from the speaker with a 1 watt input. For every doubling of power input the SPL (volume) increase by 3dB. So in this case, assuming a 100 watt power handling spec:

Power input (watts)	SPL (dB @ 1 metre)
1 watt	89
2	92
4	95
8	98
16	101
32	104
64	107
128	110

So, the SPL limit of this speaker would be somewhere between 107dB and 110dB at 1 metre.

Do I need to use the biggest amp possible?

That depends on a lot of factors such as how loud you like to listen, how quiet or noisy your car is and how many other speakers and amps are being used in the system. For example, a speaker rated 20 watts minimum and 100 watts maximum (peak) used in a convertible car driven by a 20 year-old hip-hop fan would work best with a 100-watt amp. In a BMW 5 Series driven by a jazz-loving stockbroker, that same speaker would be just as happy with a 40-watt amp.

Subwoofers

A great sound system is pleasing to the ear and is the only way to accurately replicate what the artist has intended for the listener to hear. But, as anyone who has attended a high-energy live performance can attest, there is no substitute for being able to *feel* the music. The addition of a subwoofer (or more than one) to bring out the low frequencies will add that extra dimension!

Subwoofer basics

A subwoofer is a driver that handles frequencies below the reach of regular woofers or mids - the frequencies below approximately 125 Hz. Subwoofers also free-up the other speakers in the system to do their jobs the way they were meant to, without being bothered by frequencies they couldn't possibly deliver. This means that the other speakers in the system will project better and be less prone to distortion.

Some subwoofers are self-powered and don't require an amplifier. Non-self-powered subs will require an amp, though. Additionally, a subwoofer needs a crossover to filter out the frequencies that are beyond its range of reasonable operation. Some subs have built-in crossovers, but some require separate crossovers to be properly wired into the system. For more information on crossovers, see the previous chapter.

Subwoofers are usually sold as a stand-alone item, but in just about all applications they will have to be mounted in some type of enclosure. There are many types of enclosures, designed to manipulate the acoustics of the subwoofer(s) depending on the type of vehicle in which it is being installed or the type of music that will be listened to mostly. The physics behind these various designs is not easy to understand and is way beyond the scope of this manual, so as far as installation goes, we'll deal with the most common type - the sealed enclosure.

Sealed enclosures are airtight and produce a tight and accurate bass. These enclosures are relatively easy to design and construct. By purchasing the correct driver and following the manufacturer's instructions for achieving the correct internal volume, you'll be on the way to having a subwoofer box that tends to have a more versatile bass range for all types of music.

Here are some things to think about to help you plan your addition:

Mounting location - This is probably the single most important factor when it comes to installing a sub; how much room are you willing to sacrifice? Some manufacturers offer modular subwoofer enclosures that are vehicle-specific and designed to fill unneeded voids in the interior, and this is the most hassle-free option. If space is not a problem, you'll then have to determine what kind of sound you're after, which will force you to make another decision - what kind of enclosure will you be using? If you're going with a sealed or ported box, the space it will occupy will be the limiting factor, which will then limit your choice of subwoofer size.

Sound type - What kind of music do you listen to primarily? If you like rap or hip-hop, you'll probably want a "boomier" sound, which will lead you to a subwoofer on the larger side. The cone on a big sub travels farther than the cone on a smaller one, and has a slower response time which gives you a heavier sound but a bit of distortion as well. If you like a "tighter," more accurate punch, a smaller sub will better fit your needs.

How many? - Again, the available space and type of sound you're after are the determining factors. If you're going after the boomy sound, one big subwoofer will probably suffice. If you want the quick response, sound quality and accuracy of a smaller sub, but want lots of it, you may want to think about adding a pair of smaller subs. Of course for some people, too much is never enough and if you're one of those, well, the sky (actually interior space) is the limit!

Amplification - Subwoofers require a lot of power to work properly. If you simply wired up a subwoofer to your head unit like a regular speaker it wouldn't function nearly like it should, and would probably lead you to turn up the volume in an attempt to get it "on the same page" as the rest of the speakers. Doing this would most likely damage your speakers. So, once you've decided on what type of subwoofer setup you want, you'll have to look at the power requirements furnished by the manufacturer of the subs, then go amp shopping too! Keep in mind that powered subwoofers (with a built-in amplifier) are available.

One more thing to think about - you're probably not the first person to install a subwoofer setup in a vehicle like the one you have. Talking to other enthusiasts and visiting some stereo shops will definitely shed some light on this dilemma of what you actually need to get the sound you want.

Enclosure types

There are many different types of enclosures designed to perform in different ways and highlight different parts of the low-end spectrum. No one style of enclosure will be the best design for all music genres, so you really need to come to terms with what sound you're after and what kind of space you have to work with. Here's a rundown of some of the more popular sub boxes out there:

Free air - This is actually not a box that you have to buy or build. In this setup the boot of your vehicle becomes the enclosure, and the subwoofer(s) mount to the underside of the parcel shelf or to a board fastened to the structural member behind the rear seat. With this arrangement it is very important to seal and insulate the luggage compartment, otherwise the sub(s) won't be very effective. It also requires more amplification than other enclosures, and not all subwoofers are suitable for free air mounting (the manufacturer or retailer will have that information). Properly done, you'll get good low to medium bass output and you'll still have the use of your boot.

Acoustic suspension (or sealed box) - This is the most common type of enclosure and the easiest to build. It isn't just a box that you hammer together with nails and bolt the sub into, however. The dimensions must be calculated to match the subwoofer(s) for it to work properly, and it must be thoroughly sealed. Mounting direction isn't all that important, unless the subs are firing at a surface that will cause sound waves to bounce back and cancel them out. Where a sealed box falls short is on the extreme low end (below 30 Hz), so if you're after that boomy, exaggerated bass, this might not be what you want.

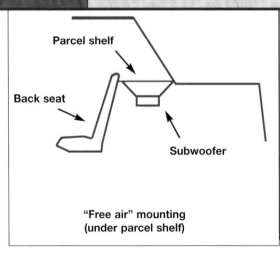

"Free air" mounting
(under parcel shelf)

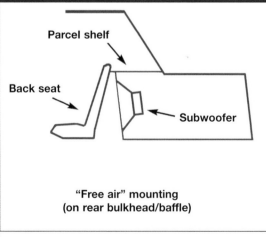

"Free air" mounting
(on rear bulkhead/baffle)

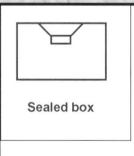

Sealed box

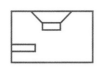

Ported box

Single reflex band pass

Bass reflex (or ported box) - This type of enclosure is similar to a sealed box, except that it has a hole in it, and a tube mounted in the hole. The port is tuned by increasing or decreasing the diameter and length of the tube. A good ported box is difficult to build (computer programs are available to help you figure out the proper dimensions of the box and port size and length) and has a response time slower than that of a sealed box. They usually have to be bigger than a sealed box for a similar subwoofer, but they also tend to be louder (and "boomier"). When mounting the box it's important not to block the port.

Bass tubes - These are essentially a bass reflex box in the form of a convenient, easily mountable tube. Some are even disguised to look like a nitrous oxide tank! (see photo above).

Single reflex band pass - This is a combination of a sealed box and a ported box; one chamber is completely sealed and the other is ported. This type of box is also difficult to build, but is efficient (low and loud bass) and smaller in size than a sealed or ported box.

Push/pull isobaric (or clamshell box) - This is essentially a sealed box with one subwoofer mounted inside and one subwoofer mounted outside, facing the other. This arrangement won't double your bass output just because your using two subs, but it will give you good bass response in a physically smaller enclosure. When wiring-up the two subs it is essential that one is wired in polarity and the other wired out of polarity (so they both travel in the same direction) - otherwise they would simply destroy each other!

*An important consideration with any type of subwoofer setup is that the sub and box must be securely mounted! Subs are heavy and you would **NOT** want one flying around inside your vehicle in the event of an accident or sudden manoeuvre.*

Push/pull (clamshell) box

Building a
sealed enclosure

First you'll have to locate a good spot for your subwoofer enclosure. Find the largest, out-of-the-way space you can, then take some measurements of that area - length, width and height. Calculate the volume of that area in cubic metres by multiplying the length x width x height in cm, then divide by 1,000,000 (this calculation is for one subwoofer; if you're building the enclosure for two subs, you'll have to halve the enclosure's volume). Be sure to allow for the thickness of the material (in the procedure that follows we'll be using 18 mm MDF, so you'll have to subtract 3.6 cm from each dimension). Now that you have an idea of what the volume of your enclosure will be, you can go shopping for a subwoofer whose enclosure volume requirements will be compatible with your available space.

Note:
Some volumes are specified in litres. Take the measurements in cm and divide by 1,000.

05 Join the remaining side panels; be sure to first run a bead of glue along the edges of the adjoining seams

06 To prevent any air leaks, seal all the seams inside the box with a silicone sealant

02 Pre-drill the screw holes to prevent the screws from splitting the panels when assembling the box

Warning!
Wear a filtering mask before cutting; MDF gives off an extremely fine dust which can be harmful to your health.

03 Run a bead of wood glue along the adjoining seams before assembling them with screws

04 Join the top panel to the rear panel. Carefully align the seam then, using screws, join the rear panel to the bottom panel

Note:
To make the assembly easier, a nail gun can be used to tack the boards together, as shown here, using screws to join them together.

07 Trace an outline of the template supplied with the subwoofer onto the front panel. Be sure to centre the cutout(s)

08 Using a jigsaw, carefully cut the holes for the subwoofers

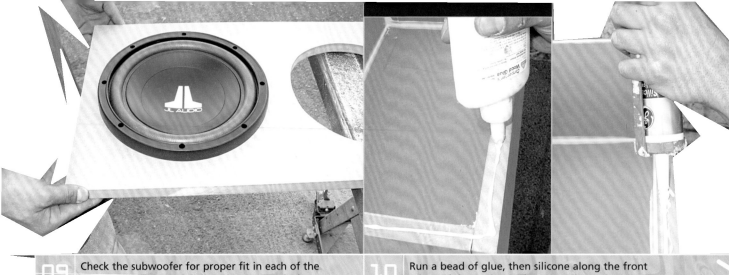

09 Check the subwoofer for proper fit in each of the cutouts. The subwoofer should be a snug fit for a good seal

10 Run a bead of glue, then silicone along the front edges of the enclosure (we're applying the silicone here because it would be difficult to do it from inside the box, working through the holes)

12 Get a large piece of carpet and cut it roughly to size. Attach the carpet to the box using a spray glue and trim off any excess, then use a razor blade to cut out the holes

13 Drill a hole for the speaker wire, then feed enough wire through for connection to the subwoofers

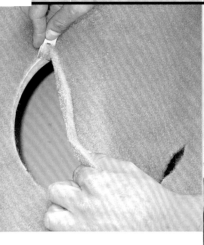

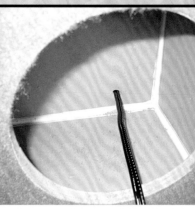

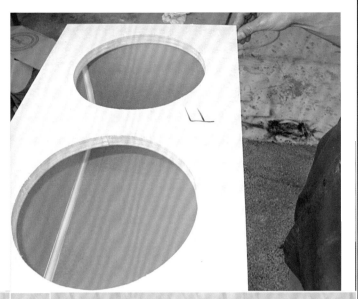

11 Align and attach the front panel to the box

Sub box hint

Insulating a sealed or ported subwoofer enclosure with poly-fill insulation will give you a bigger-sounding box. It does this by dampening the sound waves that are generated behind the subwoofer that would otherwise work against the movement of the speaker cone. If you're adding this to a ported box you'll have to devise some way of keeping the poly-fill inside so it doesn't blow out through the port.

14 Using a hot glue gun, seal the hole where the wire comes into the box

15 Follow the manufacturer's instructions for connecting the subwoofer wiring, then place them into the enclosure and mount them, also according to the manufacturer's instructions

16 Be sure to bolt the sub box down so it doesn't slide around. A loose enclosure can be dangerous, particularly in a crash. The last thing you want during an accident is half a ton of unhappy speaker and box hurtling towards you!

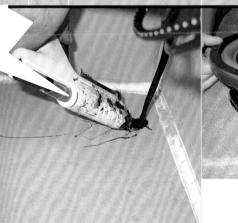

Building a
fibreglass enclosure

01 The boot area was stripped of the spare tyre to make room for the enclosure and a support frame was constructed of 18 mm Medium Density Fibreboard (MDF)

02 Next it was time to measure and cut the rings for the subs

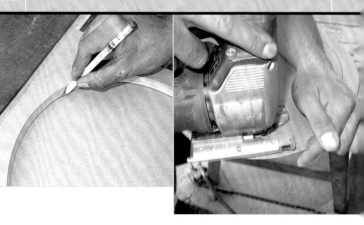

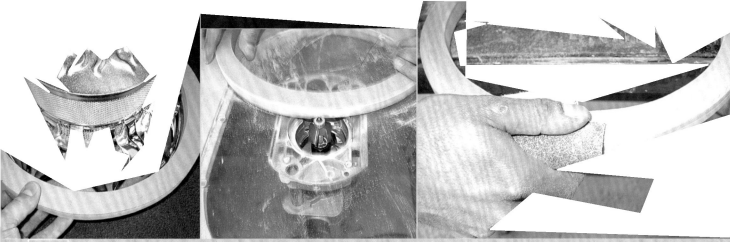

03 The rings are tried on for size, then taken to a router and some sanding to smooth out the rough edges. Wear a filtering mask before cutting MDF; it gives off an extremely fine dust which can be harmful to your health

04 Next, the supports for the sub rings are fastened to the frame using a nail gun; the rings can now be mounted >

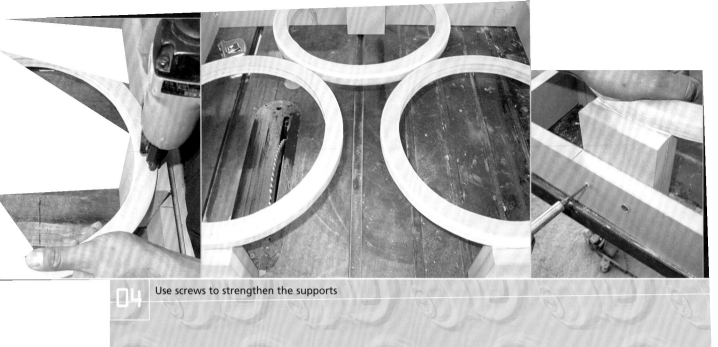

04 Use screws to strengthen the supports

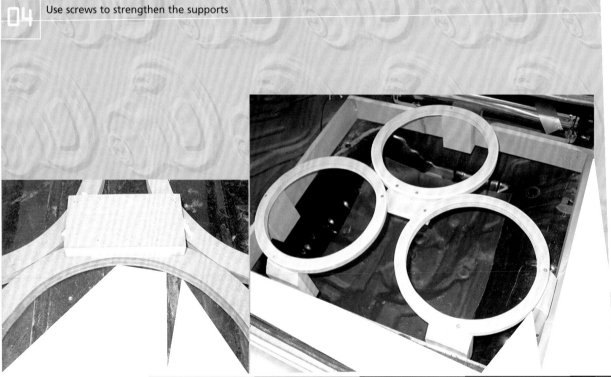

05 The rings are tied in the centre by a piece of MDF glued to the bottom, then secured by screws through the top

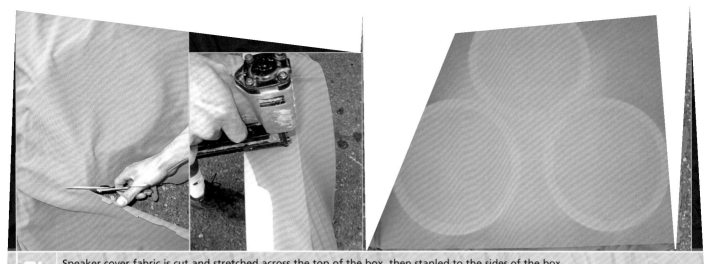

Speaker cover fabric is cut and stretched across the top of the box, then stapled to the sides of the box.

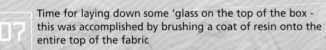

07   Time for laying down some 'glass on the top of the box - this was accomplished by brushing a coat of resin onto the entire top of the fabric

08   After a few hours of drying time . . .

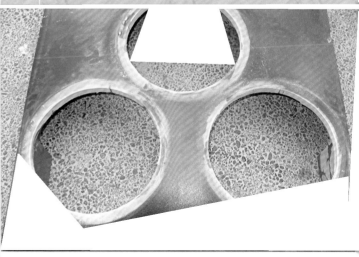

09 . . . the box is turned over, layered with fibreglass mat and brushed with resin

10 More drying time, then the inside is reinforced with steel mesh and body-filler

All-Purpose Fiberglass Resin

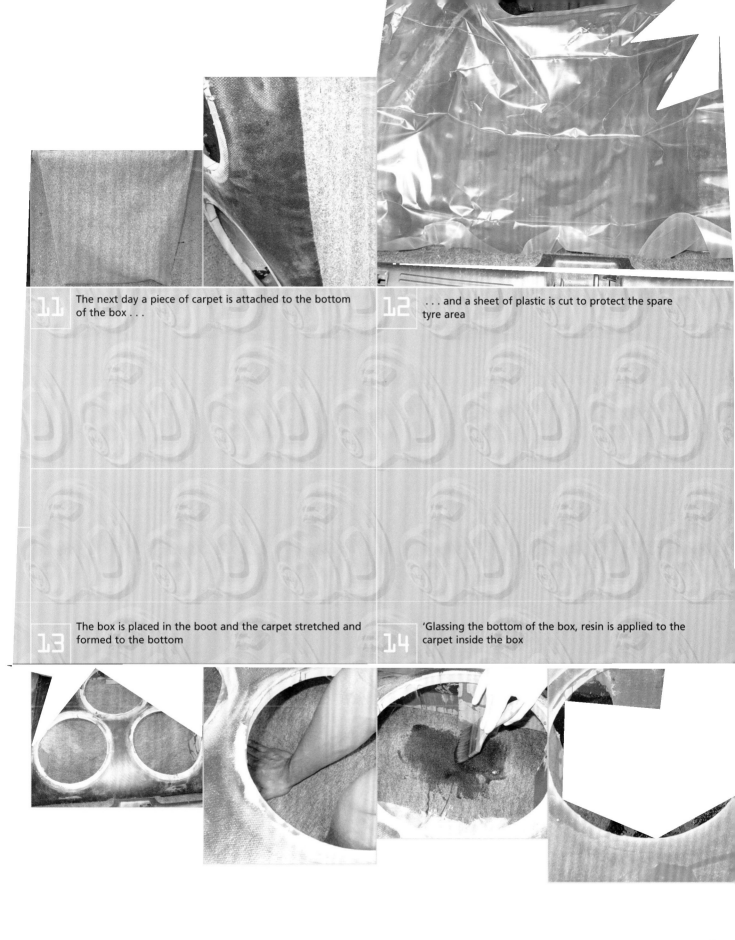

11 The next day a piece of carpet is attached to the bottom of the box . . .

12 . . . and a sheet of plastic is cut to protect the spare tyre area

13 The box is placed in the boot and the carpet stretched and formed to the bottom

14 'Glassing the bottom of the box, resin is applied to the carpet inside the box

15 After several hours of drying time, the box is removed from the boot and the top of the box is sanded. Be sure to wear the proper mask and eye protection

16 Then a coat of body filler is added to fill in any imperfections . . .

17 . . . and smoothed out with a surform and sandpaper.

18 A coat of primer is applied to the top . . .

19 . . . then sanded for a smooth surface that's ready for the paint shop

20 A few last things before painting: the subs get checked for fit and the holes are pre-drilled

21 After returning from the paint shop the box is placed in its final resting spot, then the subs are wired up and mounted. *Look out, eardrums!*

Vehicle specific
enclosures

Some manufacturers offer ready-made, vehicle-specific sub-box enclosures. These are a convenient alternative for people not willing or able to construct a box, or for those who want a more factory look, sacrificing as little interior space as possible.

01 Handcrafted from fibreglass, the JL Audio Stealthbox will convert our centre seat cushion and folding armrest into a sealed, downfiring subwoofer enclosure

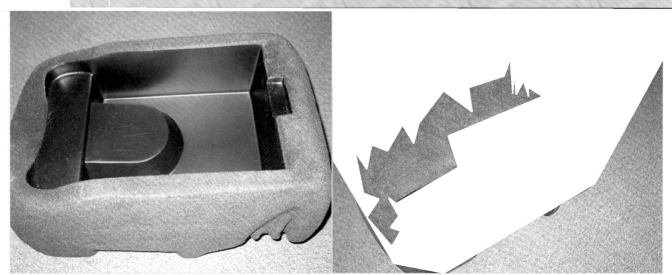

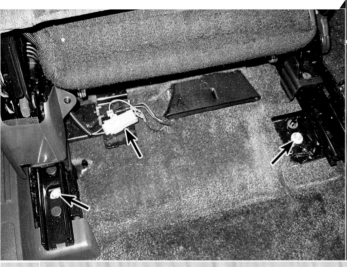

02 The first thing to go is the seats. Most of the time, removing the seat is a simple matter of removing the four bolts securing the seat to the floorpan and lifting the seat from the vehicle. You may also have to disconnect an electrical connector or two. If your vehicle is equipped with side-impact airbags and/or seat belt pre-tensioners, you'll have to disable the airbag system (refer to the Haynes Service and Repair Manual for your vehicle)

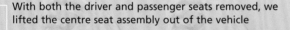

03 With both the driver and passenger seats removed, we lifted the centre seat assembly out of the vehicle

04 Following the installation guide, we disassembled the factory centre-seat cushion and the upper storage tray. We saved all the upper tray's parts for use during reassembly

05 The centre seat frame needed a bit of modification. Referring to the illustrations in the installation guide, we drilled each hole then checked the fit of the frame by placing it on the bottom of the Stealthbox

06 The frame was a perfect fit, so we attached it to the bottom of the Stealthbox with the supplied hardware

07 Before proceeding further, we attached speaker wires to the Stealthbox and tested its operation

08 Following the installation guide, we reassembled the latch, then secured the tray to the Stealthbox with the supplied hardware

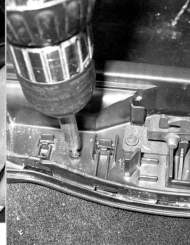

09 The Stealthbox was placed in the vehicle and the speaker wires were connected

10 Before installing the driver's seat we ran the speaker wire under the carpet so it could eventually be connected to the amplifier

11 The seats were installed to complete the installation. The finished Stealthbox is a perfect match to the factory interior and sounds great!

FAQs
Subwoofers

How big should my subwoofer enclosure be?

Information for matching the enclosure's size to the speaker's parameters should be included in the speaker's manual. Also, many speaker manufacturers provide this information on their websites.

When I construct my enclosure, what materials should I use?

Medium Density Fiberboard (MDF) is a good all around choice, easy to cut. Just be sure to wear a filtering mask (you don't want to breathe the dust from this stuff!).

What should I use to seal the enclosure?

Start by gluing all connecting edges, then use screws to complete the job. Finish it off by using silicone sealant along all of the interior joints.

What type of glue should I use?

A good wood glue is a safe choice.

What kind of silicone sealant should I use?

The same kind that you'd use for sealing a bathtub or shower (just make sure it's silicone sealant, not caulking compound).

How long should I let the glue and sealant cure before mounting the subs?

24 hours, because some chemicals may damage the some of the materials used in the woofers. And you want to make sure everything is completely dry and set-up, because the subs are going to generate a lot of pressure inside of the box.

How many screws do I need to hold the connecting edges?

Try using 60 mm screws every 100 mm.

How do I prevent the wood from splitting when using screws to fasten the boards?

Pre-drill the holes first.

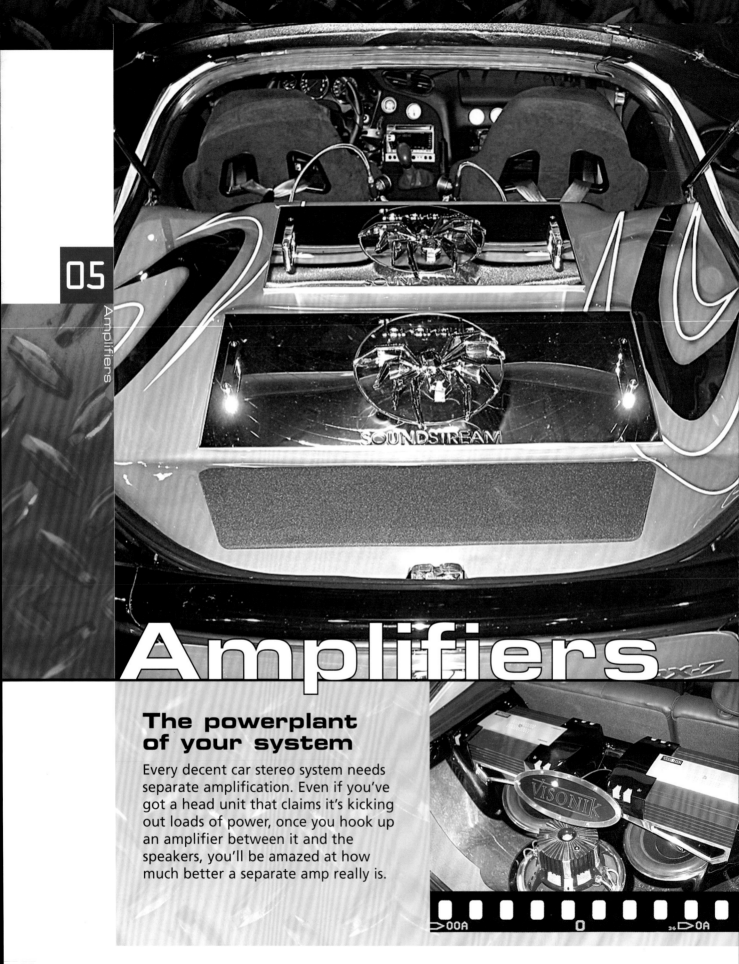

Amplifiers

The powerplant of your system

Every decent car stereo system needs separate amplification. Even if you've got a head unit that claims it's kicking out loads of power, once you hook up an amplifier between it and the speakers, you'll be amazed at how much better a separate amp really is.

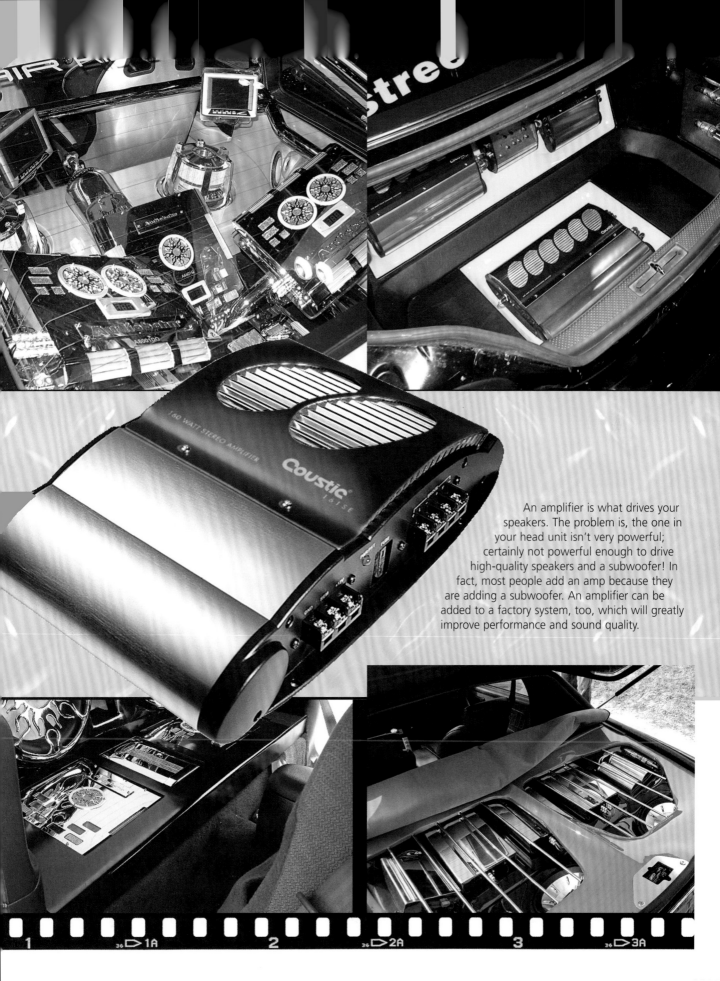

An amplifier is what drives your speakers. The problem is, the one in your head unit isn't very powerful; certainly not powerful enough to drive high-quality speakers and a subwoofer! In fact, most people add an amp because they are adding a subwoofer. An amplifier can be added to a factory system, too, which will greatly improve performance and sound quality.

When wiring up an amplifier, it's very important to do everything properly. The amplifier power wire must have a fuse mounted somewhere close to the battery, and be sure to use a grommet to protect the wire where it enters the passenger compartment. The signal cable from the head unit to the amplifier should be routed away from the car's wiring as well as the amplifier's power wire so that it doesn't pick up any nasty noise.

Lead photo: This amplifier fits nicely under the rear fold-up seat

Bottom and right: Amplifier wiring kits like these are available for making the job of installation easy

When the music is turned up and the car lights go dim, maybe an external capacitor is needed. External capacitors store power between the amplifier and the battery, providing extra power when necessary, eliminating an unnecessary strain on the vehicle's alternator or battery

How an
amp works

The amplifier takes a signal and makes it larger without adding to, or taking away from, the original signal. To do this, the amplifier needs a power supply with a size proportional to the expected output. The car provides the amp with 12 volts in DC. The audio output will be in AC. The power supply of the amplifier takes the 12 volts from the car and steps it up. The voltage is increased substantially. The positive side will push the speaker and the negative side will pull the speaker as it reproduces music.

MOSFETs (Metal-Oxide Semiconductor Field Effect Transistors) are typically used in the power supply, and this is an acronym you should look for when shopping for an amp. MOSFETs can control much more current than traditional FETs (Field Effect Transistors). This additional current handling allows amplifiers to operate at lower impedances over a greater temperature range.

Impedance is the resistance of a speaker to AC (music is alternating current). While 4 ohms is typical for car audio speakers, some applications call for putting two speakers in parallel, creating a 2-ohm circuit. Ohm's Law tells us that when the resistance falls, the power goes up. So the amplifier will attempt to produce more power when a low impedance is presented. The MOSFET technology helps the amp's power supply meet this demand.

Some signal wires include a remote turn-on wire

Channels

Anywhere from one to eight channels of amplified output are available. The number of amplifier channels is just as important as the output power for determining the right amp for your needs. Channels can be configured in different ways for different applications. For example, a four-channel amplifier can have two channels bridged while the remaining two channels operate in stereo. This creates a three-channel system. A two-channel amp can drive two speakers in stereo, while a third (subwoofer) is bridged across the right and left channels. A six-channel amplifier can have two channels bridged while the remaining four operate in stereo. Any number of combinations can be accomplished with multi-channel amps. For example, a four-channel amp is used in three-channel mode, where the low-pass crossover (which lets only the low frequencies through) sends bass to the mono channel for subwoofer input, while the remaining stereo signal is used to drive a pair of components in the doors in a high-pass mode.

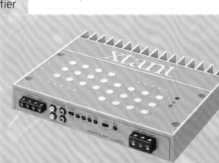

What is bridging?

Bridging an amplifier involves using the left and right channel together to drive one or more speakers. Most modern 12V amplifiers are capable of being bridged. This process combines two channels to produce a higher power output to a single speaker or a group of speakers. Most (but not all) amplifiers today are made to be bridged. Caution: Amplifier manufacturers provide information on a stable limit for impedance in a bridged mode. For example, if an amplifier is only stable to 2 ohms in bridged mode, it is imperative that the speaker system does not present a load that is lower than 2 ohms.

Classes

There are different types of amplifiers. Amplifier classes indicate an amplifier's efficiency and sound quality. Typically, the more efficient the amplifier, the poorer the sound quality. For example, a high-power head unit has a very high-efficiency amplifier but is not known for its sound quality. If the output current flows over a longer amount of the cycle, the amplifier will be less efficient. On the other hand, if the output current flows over a shorter amount of the cycle, the amplifier will be more efficient.

In simpler terms, if an amp uses 100 watts of battery power, but puts out only 50 watts, it is said to be 50% efficient. If it uses 100 watts of battery power, but puts out 80, then its about 80% efficient.

Class A: A Class A amplifier has a clean output, but poor efficiency. Most Class A amplifiers operate at about 20% to 30% efficiency. For example, if the amp requires about 100 watts of input power from the battery, it will only output about 20 to 30 watts of audio signal to the speakers.

Class B: This class of amps has twice the efficiency of Class A amps. Even though Class B amps might seem ideal, they cause audio distortion and are rarely used in car audio.

Class AB: Probably the most common 12V amplifier today, this amp provides good sound quality while maintaining efficiency. Most car audio amplifiers use a Class AB design.

Class D: The Class D amp is very efficient, but requires a complex output filter, which increases cost. The efficiency is due to the power supply following the input signal and adjusting itself accordingly. The Class D amplifier switches on and off hundreds of thousands of times per second. Class D is not a designation for Digital, as some literature may have you believe.

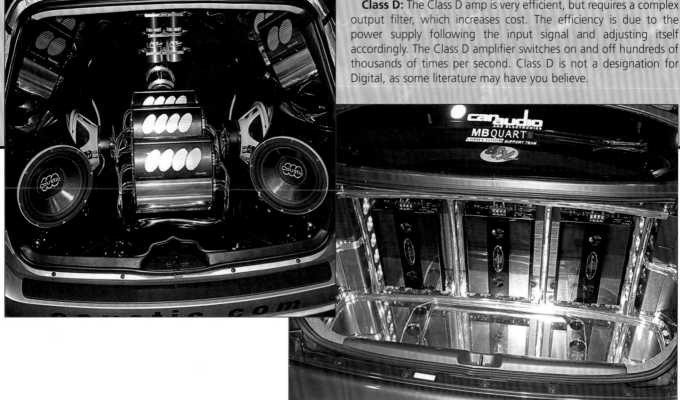

Choosing the
right amp

The first step is to determine the needs of your system. If you're just adding an amp to improve your original equipment system, you may need only minimal amplification. Therefore, a small inexpensive amp will suffice. On the other hand, if you're planning on running multiple subwoofers and component speakers, you'll most likely need multiple amplifiers.

Next, you have to figure out if you need an amplifier with a built-in crossover or an amp that is dedicated to playing a full-range signal. A built-in crossover can cross over different frequencies dedicated to a particular speaker, whereas a 12-inch subwoofer will sound best playing 100Hz and down. This will maximise the life of the speaker playing in this frequency range.

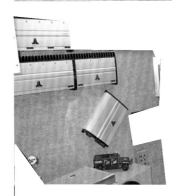

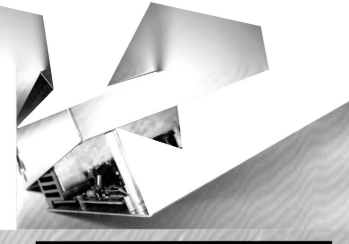

How powerful of an amp does your system need? Well, that depends what kind and how many speakers it has to drive. The amp should be capable of putting out 1-1/2 to two times the power (continuous, or RMS power in watts) that the lowest-frequency speaker that it'll be driving is rated. The specifications you'll find when shopping for an amp will indicate how many watts-per-channel the amp is able to produce continuously. This sounds weird, but an underpowered amp can actually damage your speakers when the volume is turned up. The waveform it puts out changes from a nice curvy sine wave into more of a square wave, which speakers don't like; this is called *clipping*, because the top and bottom of the wave gets "clipped" off. The speakers can handle the extra power better than they can this ugly square wave.

Finally, how many channels must the amplifier have in order to interface with the stereo system? Say, for example, you're running four speakers and you want to add amplifiers to enhance the sound. You must decide if you want to retain the use of the fader. If you do, you will need to purchase a four-channel amplifier with four independent RCA inputs. A four-channel amplifier can run four speakers in a stereo fashion without losing fading capability.

Amplifiers

When installing the amplifier's power wire, how close to the battery should I install a fuse or circuit breaker?

As close to the battery as possible. The professional standard for fusing a power cable is no less than 25 cm from the battery terminal, but no further than 46 cm.

What is the minimum distance I should keep my signal wires separated from any power wires?

A minimum of 46 cm should separate power from signal.

Where can I mount my amplifier?

Generally an amplifier can be mounted anywhere there's room. Under a seat or in the boot are good locations as long as there's adequate ventilation. Mounting an amplifier upside down under something is not a good idea, though; as the amplifier produces heat, the heat will rise and have nowhere to go.

Where can I earth my amplifier?

The closer to the amplifier the better. This will help prevent any noise entering the system. Use a good ring terminal and be sure the contact point is free of rust and/or paint.

What size power cable should I use for my amp?

Follow the manufacturer's instructions included with the amp. Also take a look at the amplifier power cable chart later in this Chapter.

When installing multiple amps in my system, should I run a power cable for each amp to the battery?

One power wire connected at the battery should connect to a power distribution block. Separate power wires from each amp should then connect to the power distribution block.

Should I replace the factory battery cable clamp?

Yes. You will need to connect a power wire from the amp. A terminal clamp with an auxiliary adapter would be ideal.

What is the best way for connecting wires in the engine compartment?

Soldering the connection is best, and be sure to follow it with heat shrink tubing to insulate the connection and protect the joint from corrosion.

What if I have to run a wire through a hole in the body?

Always use a grommet.

What is a capacitor's purpose in a sound system?

The capacitors primary responsibility is to add stored energy to assist the vehicle's electrical system, based on how much current the amplifier needs. This provides for a more stable voltage supply and, in turn, enables the amplifier to run more efficiently.

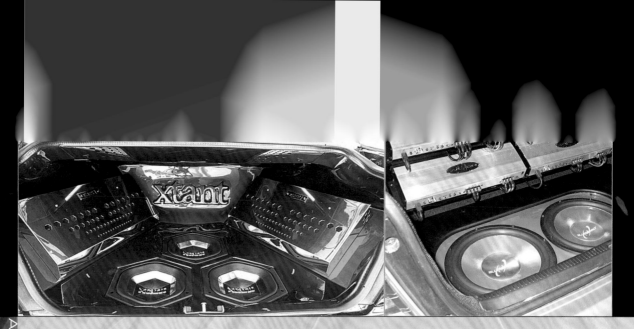

Upgrading
considerations

Once you're familiar with what an amplifier can do, you may want to upgrade to a better amplifier or buy one that has more features. The number-one reason to upgrade to a better amplifier would be to have more power. High-pass, low-pass, and bandpass internal crossovers are another common amplifier feature. If you're adding a subwoofer to a factory system, then an amplifier with some type of low-pass crossover to block the high frequency from the subwoofer is needed.

Another upgrading consideration would be the number of channels the amplifier might have. If you already have an amplifier operating two rear speakers, you may want to introduce more power to the front speakers. Upgrading to a four-channel amplifier to run the front and rear speakers would be an ideal way to make this improvement. Another alternative would be to simply add a second amp to drive the front speakers.

Size is a very important consideration when upgrading. Many enthusiasts want amps that can easily mount out of the way, under seats, walls, and floors of boots.

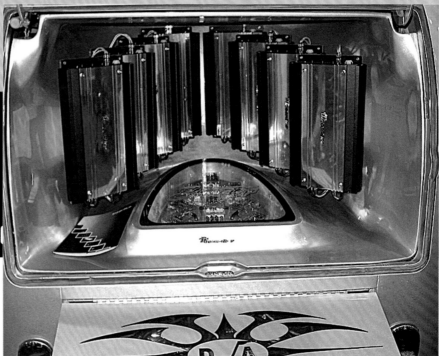

Using amplifiers
effectively

Once an amplifier is installed, the level of the amp must be adjusted to match the rest of the system. The ideal setting is one where the maximum signal is being fed to the amplifier while introducing zero distortion. Some amplifiers have clip indicators, which illuminate when the input level is too high. If the gain control is too low, then one must turn the volume of the radio up. This will amplify unwanted noises at this volume.

To improve the performance of some amplifiers, a stiffening capacitor can be added. A capacitor stores current, and when the amplifier demands more current (like when the subwoofer kicks in real hard) it will pull it from the capacitor(s) instantly. This will result in increased performance from the amplifier. The capacitor must be placed as close as possible to the amplifier if it is to work properly. The size of the amp would determine the size capacitor to use. It is recommended to use 100,000 microfarads per 100 watts of power.

The condition of the vehicle's battery and alternator are also important to amplifier performance. If the amp isn't being fed what it needs, it can't possibly put out what you want.

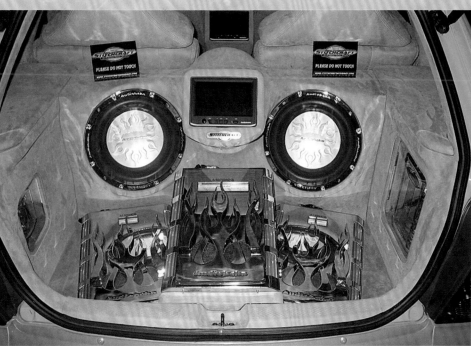

Other items you'll need for amplifier installation

In addition to the amplifier(s), here are some items that you should pick up before you go back home to do the install:

- **Wire and cable** - Figure out how much cabling you need to connect your new amp to the battery, and how much speaker wire, also. Now would be the best time to upgrade your standard speaker wire to heavy-gauge speaker wire.

- **Connectors and solder** - Calculate how many connectors you'll need to hook up your amps and speakers, then buy a few more just in case. If you're using any connectors which require solder, use only resin core solder.

- **Shrink tubing** - If you're using connectors that have to be soldered to the wire or cable, get some shrink tubing to cover your solder joints. It makes for a much cleaner-looking installation than electrician's tape, not to mention a more secure and longer-lasting one.

- **Fuse holder** - Get a fuse holder with amperage rating high enough for your setup. This will have to be installed in the power cable, as close to the battery as possible.

- **Battery terminal** - Since you're going to be running a heavy-gauge cable from your positive battery post to the amplifier, get a new battery terminal with provisions for attaching one or more additional cable to it (if the terminal you have won't accept another cable).

- **Grommet** - If you have to drill a new hole in the bulkhead for your amp's power cable, this will protect it from chafing through the insulation and shorting out.

- **Power distribution block** - If you're installing more than one amplifier you'll need one of these.

- **Mounting hardware** - What kind you'll need depends on where and how you'll be mounting the amp, but pick up everything you think you'll need before you actually start the job.

Note:
Many retailers sell amplifier installation kits that contain most of the items you'll need.

Amplifier mounting tips

An amplifier can generally be mounted anywhere there's room, as long as it isn't in a harsh environment or an area where it would get too hot. Under a seat is a good location as long as there is adequate airspace above the top of the amp, and so is in the boot. The one thing you don't want to do is mount the amp to the underside of something, such as underneath the parcel shelf. This could cause the amp to overheat, because heat rises and in this case would have nowhere to go.

Always secure the amp properly, using any brackets that were supplied with the amp, and good quality fasteners. Make sure the surface that the amp is mounted to will support the weight of the amp, and won't "let go" of it in the event of an accident.

Whenever it becomes necessary to drill through the floor or a panel of the vehicle to mount an amp, make sure there's nothing on the other side that could be damaged by the drill bit or by the fastener that will be screwed into the hole.

Always use high-quality connectors. If you're using ring-type connectors, it's a good idea to solder them to the wire or cable to ensure a good connection that won't corrode. Tighten all fasteners securely.

Whenever you have to run a cable or wire through the bulkhead or other body panel, be sure to insulate the hole with a grommet. This is imperative, since it will prevent the wire's insulation from rubbing through and shorting out, which could cause a fire.

The fuse in the amplifier's power cable must be located as close to the battery as possible, and the fuse's amperage rating must be equal to or less than the amplifier's fuse(s).

The amplifier must be securely earthed, using the same gauge cable as the power cable. The amp's earth cable should be as short as possible; ideally, less than 46 cm.

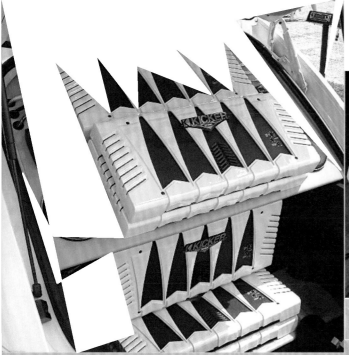

01 Deciding where the amplifier is going to be installed is the first step. In this case, we've opted for mounting it under the front seat

Installing an
amplifier

Amplifier power cable chart (SWG)

To avoid excessive voltage drop, be sure to use the proper gauge cable to power your amp(s). Remember, an amp needs a good voltage supply to work properly, so don't skimp in this department!

Current draw (in amps)	Distance from battery to amp						
	0 to 120 cm	120 to 210 cm	210 to 300 cm	300 to 400 cm	400 to 500 cm	500 to 670 cm	670 to 850 cm
0 to 20	16	14	14	12	12	10	10
20 to 35	14	12	10	10	8	8	5
35 to 50	12	10	10	8	5	5	5
50 to 65	10	10	8	5	5	5	3
65 to 85	8	8	5	5	3	3	0
85 to 105	8	8	5	3	3	3	0
105 to 125	5	5	5	3	0	0	0
125 to 150	3	3	3	0	0	0	000

02 Most of the time, removing the seat is a simple matter of removing the four bolts securing the seat to the floorpan and lifting the seat from the vehicle. You may also have to disconnect an electrical connector or two. If your vehicle is equipped with side-impact airbags, you'll have to disable the airbag system (refer to the Haynes Service and Repair Manual for your vehicle)

03 Running the amplifier's power wire starts at the battery. The main power wire needs to have a waterproof fuse holder mounted as close to the battery as possible

04 Use a short piece of power wire between the battery and the fuse holder

> ⚠️ **Warning:**
> Whenever working on a vehicle equipped with an airbag (or airbags), be sure to disable the airbag system before working in the vicinity of any airbag system components. This is especially important when working around the instrument panel and centre console. Consult the Haynes Service and Repair Manual for your vehicle for the airbag disabling procedure. If no manual exists, consult a dealer service department or other qualified repair shop to obtain the information. Also, NEVER splice or tap into any wiring for the airbag system, and never use a test light or multimeter on airbag system wiring. On most vehicles the wiring for the airbag system is yellow, or is covered by yellow conduit, or at the very least will have yellow electrical connectors.

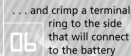

05 Attach the other half of the fuse holder to one end of the short power wire . . .

06 . . . and crimp a terminal ring to the side that will connect to the battery

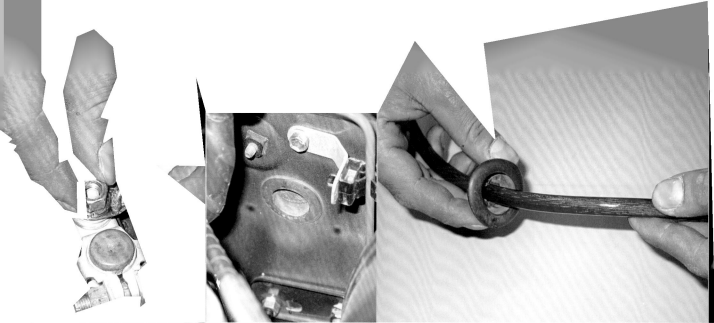

07 Connecting the power wire at the terminal is ok, just be sure NOT to install a fuse and complete the power connection until you finish the entire installation

08 The power wire now needs to be routed to the passenger compartment. How to get the wire through the bulkhead doesn't have to be a dilemma - just find an existing hole like this one . . .

09 . . . remove the grommet, cut a small hole in it and feed the power wire through the grommet and bulkhead. Be sure to refit the grommet to the bulkhead to prevent water leaks and to protect the wire

10 Inside the engine compartment, use split loom to cover and protect the entire power wire

11 Using wire ties helps keep the tubing from sliding off

12 Inside the passenger compartment, properly secure the power wire to prevent being tangled or getting in the way of the pedals

13 The carpet is pulled back and the wire is directed towards the amplifier's mounting location

Note:
When routing the signal cables, keep them a minimum 46 cm from any power wire including any vehicle wiring harness

14 The amplifier's remote turn on wire and signal cable have to be connected at the back of the stereo head. Route the remote turn on wire in the direction of the amplifier's power wire where it enters at the bulkhead.

15 Route the amp's power wire and remote turn on wire together under the carpet - use wire ties or electrical tape to keep them tidy

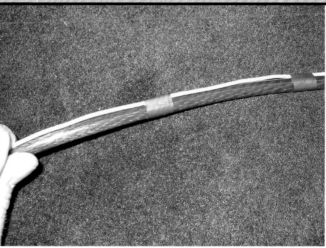

16 At the amplifier, a power distribution block can be used if two amplifiers are being installed

17 After securing the main power wire . . .

18 . . . two separate smaller gauge power wires split off to supply each amplifier

19 Cut a short length of wire for the earth and crimp a ring terminal on one end. Find a spot to mount it to the vehicle chassis. Be sure to sand off any paint so that the connection is made directly to metal

20 Connect the power cable, remote turn on wire and earth wire to the amplifier. With this amplifier from JL Audio, the wires connect directly to the amp using an Allen key without the need for terminals

21 The same is done for the subwoofer speaker wires

22 Wire ties can be used to keep the power, remote and earth wires together

Note:
Always follow the manufacturer's recommendations for mounting the amplifier. Properly securing an amp is very important so that it's not sliding around. A sliding amplifier that's not properly mounted can damage the unit, or worse, be dangerous during an accident. The last thing you want during an accident is a UFO (unnecessary flying object) inside the passenger compartment!

23 Connect the signal cables to the amplifier

24 With the installation complete it's time to install the fuse and test the amplifier. Carefully follow the manufacturer's instructions for powering up the amp and making any necessary adjustments

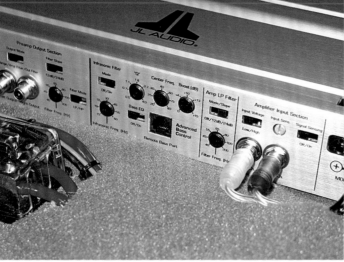
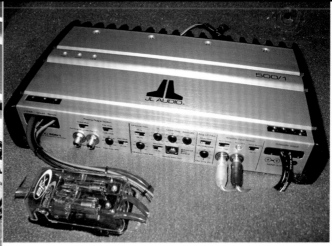

KENWOOD
music keg

POWERED BY
PHATNOISE

06

CD Changers and digital music players

CD Changers
and Digital
Music Players

The perfect companion for a long
trip, or when you just don't want to
hassle with the radio or individual
CDs or tapes, a CD changer or digital
music player stores hours of your
favorite tunes. The ultimate "front-
end" to your sound system.

Kenwood USA Corp.

CD changers

A CD changer can enhance your audio system while offering many options such as random and repeat play, and the capability of adding titles to the discs. They are fairly easy to install because their compact design allows mounting virtually anywhere in the vehicle and connection is straightforward. There are three basic types of CD changers, distinguished by how they are connected to your audio system:

- *Direct connection*
- *FM modulated (not legal in every country)*
- *Auxiliary input*

Direct connection

This installation involves connecting a cable between the CD changer to a radio head unit of the same brand (or a radio head with CD changer control capability and compatible with the CD changer). Many late-model original-equipment head units have a factory option to accept a changer.

Original equipment changer controllers typically use the same cable as their aftermarket version, making it easier to connect a compatible changer to the head unit. This type of installation is so popular that manufacturers also offer "plug and play" cable adapters compatible with the factory head units.

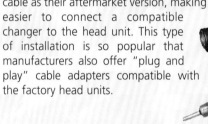

FM modulated

FM modulated (also called RF [radio frequency] modulated) CD changers are popular installations because they only involve adding a changer, an FM modulator and a remote mounted control unit. It isn't necessary to replace the factory head unit because the changer is designed to convert the CD signal to an FM frequency and play through the existing FM radio head unit.

The only drawback to the FM modulated is that sound quality is limited by the radio's reproduction ability, but the ease of installation makes this one of the most popular routes to take when choosing a CD changer.

Auxiliary (AUX) input

Because it connects by cable to an existing head unit as an additional (auxiliary) source, this is probably the easiest CD changer installation. Most of the wiring is already done because the necessary switching functions are usually built into either the head unit or a downstream pre-amp level processor.

AUX inputs sometimes have a 5-pin, 8-pin or 13-pin female DIN connector on the back of the head, and many electronics stores carry reasonably priced wiring adapters. Since the internal selector already has an AUX position for the auxiliary source, the input selector can choose between the head unit's tuner, tape or auxiliary input. The factory head unit can't control the functions of the auxiliary source, so a separate controller is required for operating the CD changer.

What should I look for?

When deciding on a CD changer you'll have to weigh its features against its price, then figure out what's best for your needs. Typically, CD changers are available in 6-disc, 10-disc and 12-disc models (those are the most common, anyway), so you'll have to determine how much music play-time and variety you want.

Once you've made that decision, check out the technical specs. Does the unit play CDs that you've burned from your home computer? Most of them do, but check to make sure - it's nice to have the ability to be able to load store-bought CDs along with CD-Rs or CD-RWs burned with MP3 files into the changer without having to think about whether or not they'll play when it's their turn!

Another convenient feature is the unit's ability to display information on the control head that mounts on the dash. This will let you know the artist and song title as the song plays.

Wireless remote - This is another good feature to have, although not completely necessary. It'll simply prevent you from having to reach up to the instrument panel to browse through your discs and tracks.

Electronic shock protection - This feature incorporates digital memory into the playback circuitry, which will ensure uninterrupted play if you hit a hard bump that would cause the CD to "jump." This is a huge improvement over the early CD changers and another attribute worth looking for.

Make sure the unit is able to be mounted where you want to put it; not just size-wise, but in its orientation. Is it able to be mounted flat as well as vertical, or somewhere in between? Figure out your mounting requirements before you start shopping.

FAQs
CD changers

What features prevent CD skip?

CD changers with Electronic Shock Protection provide a memory buffer that reads ahead and stores a bit of the information a few seconds ahead of what you're hearing.

Can I connect any aftermarket CD-changer to my factory head unit if it has CD-changer controls?

That depends on the availability of OEM interface CD changer adaptors. With some applications its as easy as connecting the CD changer's connector to the adaptor, then to the factory harness.

What if my head unit doesn't have CD-changer controls?

You can integrate an FM modulator to control the changer.

What are CD-R and CD-RWs?

With a CD-R disc the R stands for "recordable" enabling you to permanently record one time to the disc. A CD-RW disc allows the user unlimited amount of times they can record and erase information from the disc.

Can my CD player play MP3 files burned on CD-R or CD-RWs?

Only if the player is MP3 compatible and has an MP3 decoder.

This compact drive can hold the equivalent of 15 CDs of digital music

Digital music
players

The new generation of music isn't pressed onto vinyl or recorded on tape; it's digitised as a computer file and downloaded. So how do you take that music with you on the road? A digital music player for your car.

Like CD changers, digital music players also make possible the ability to carry a huge amount of music on the road, but without having to touch a single CD. Furthermore, some units allow you to organise your music in a variety of ways; by genre, artist, or album, for example. Most digital players can recognise all of the popular digital music formats.

Types of digital music players

CD/MP3 head unit

The simplest type of digital music player is a stereo head unit that plays CDs burned with MP3 music files. This is an economic way to play lots of music continuously without adding a CD changer or a remote digital music storage device.

In-dash hard drive

Another type of head unit that'll play digital music is the in-dash hard drive. Memory capacity varies amongst these units, but most will hold (at the time of writing) around 10-gigs worth of music. These units will allow you to copy music from your CDs, CD-Rs or CD-RWs right onto the hard drive. Some also have "memory stick" media which allows you to download music from your computer right into the memory stick. You then plug the memory stick into the head unit, bypassing the CD altogether.

Remotely mounted hard drive

The most popular type of add-on digital music player is the remotely mounted hard drive which connects to your system just like a CD changer. In the most common version, a removable hard drive is unplugged from the unit and plugged into a docking station connected to your home computer. You can then download music files to the drive, transfer it to the player, and take a long road trip without hearing the same song twice! Another variation of this setup works in a similar fashion but bypasses the part about transporting the hard drive from your vehicle to your home computer; it does it wirelessly. A transmitter connected to your computer will beam songs right out to the hard drive in your vehicle up to about 150 feet - even through walls!

WAV files

An uncompressed audio file format that contains CD-quality audio which require large amounts of your computer's disk space for storage.

MP3 files

Internet-standard encoding format that compresses audio into a small file for storing on a computer.

MP4 files

The latest audio file compression that resembles CD-quality when compressed at 128 kbps (stereo).

Windows Media Audio (WMA)

High-fidelity compressed music file that is smaller in file size than MP3 compression.

ATRAC 3 files (Adaptive Transform Acoustic Coding)

A Sony-developed file compression format that was first used for MiniDiscs, and now includes memory sticks and some hard-disk drives. ATRAC 3 files cannot be burned to CD-R/RW discs.

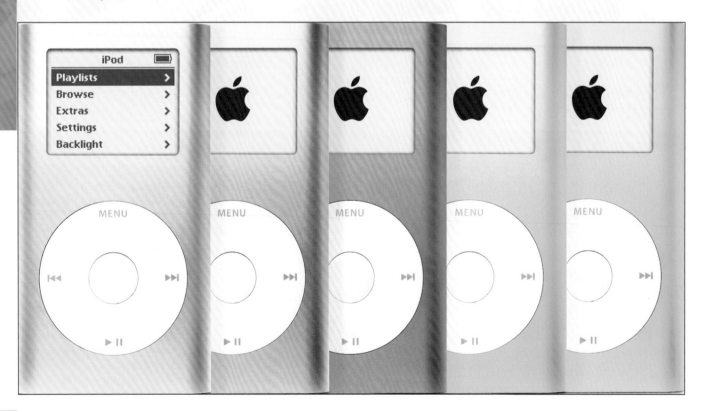

Digital music player
with an FM modulator installation

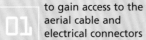
01 With the battery disconnected, remove the stereo head unit to gain access to the aerial cable and electrical connectors

02 Find a mounting location for the FM modulator (for example, under a front seat, inside or under the glove box).

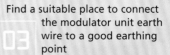
03 Find a suitable place to connect the modulator unit earth wire to a good earthing point

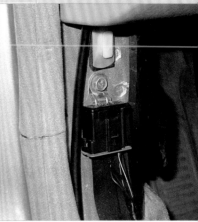

04 Use wire ties to keep wires neat and together

05 Connect the display unit cable and the digital music player cable to the modulator

06 At the back of the stereo head unit follow the manufacturer's instructions and connect the vehicle's aerial cable to the modulator's aerial input, then connect the modulator output cable to the head unit's aerial input. Mount the head unit back into the dash

Follow the manufacturer's instructions for connecting the power wires. Here we used a test light to find accessory power in the fuse box . . .

10

11 . . . then connected the B+ power and ignition (switched) wires

Connect the docking station to your PC and, using the supplied software, download your favourite tunes

12

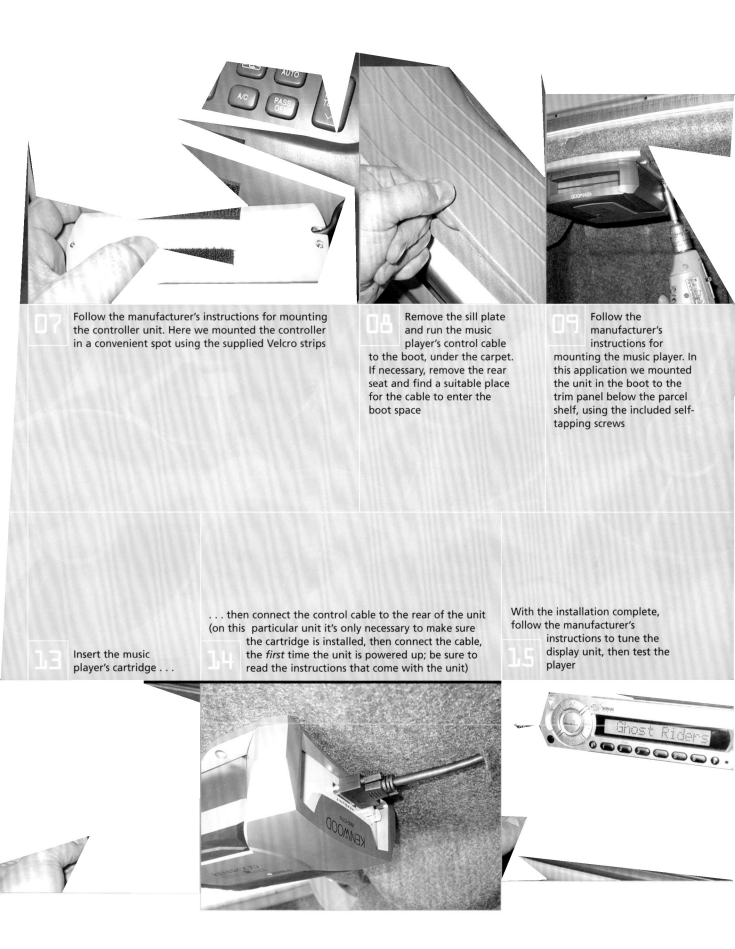

07 Follow the manufacturer's instructions for mounting the controller unit. Here we mounted the controller in a convenient spot using the supplied Velcro strips

08 Remove the sill plate and run the music player's control cable to the boot, under the carpet. If necessary, remove the rear seat and find a suitable place for the cable to enter the boot space

09 Follow the manufacturer's instructions for mounting the music player. In this application we mounted the unit in the boot to the trim panel below the parcel shelf, using the included self-tapping screws

13 Insert the music player's cartridge . . .

14 . . . then connect the control cable to the rear of the unit (on this particular unit it's only necessary to make sure the cartridge is installed, then connect the cable, the *first* time the unit is powered up; be sure to read the instructions that come with the unit)

15 With the installation complete, follow the manufacturer's instructions to tune the display unit, then test the player

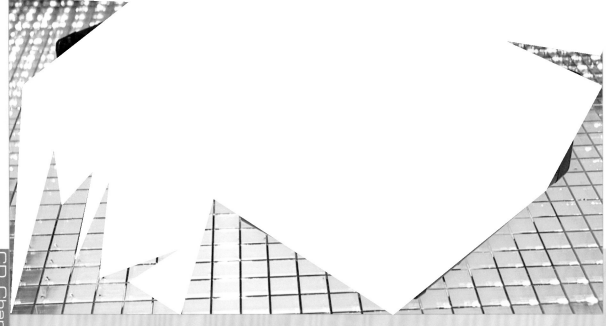

Factory CD changer installation

Many vehicles come from the factory pre-wired for a CD changer. The changer is often installed by the dealer at the time of the original sale and usually at a steep premium. But you can add your own factory changer in no time and save the installation fee in the process. So how do you know if your vehicle is pre-wired? Check the factory head unit. If it has CD controls, you probably have a wiring harness just waiting to be plugged into your new changer. Check your owner's manual to find out where the changer should be mounted and where the wires are hiding.

01 After finding the mounting location, we had to remove the boot liner and locate the factory installed signal/control cable . . .

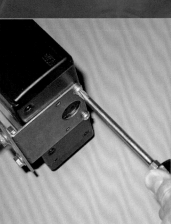

02 . . . and the power cable for the CD changer

03 Attach the mounting brackets to the sides of the changer

04 Connect the power cable . . .

05 . . . and the control cable to the CD changer

06 Carefully lower the changer into the mounting location and install the mounting screws into the pre-punched holes

07 Reinstall the boot liner.

08 Check to see if the changer's magazine can be inserted and removed smoothly from the changer

CD Changers and digital music players

CD changer with an FM modulator installation

01 With the battery disconnected, remove the stereo head unit and disconnect the aerial and power connectors

02 Find a suitable mounting location for the FM modulator (for example; under a front seat, inside or under the glove box). With this vehicle, the modulator is being mounted in the space below the radio, behind the instrument panel structure

03 Mark, then carefully drill the holes for the modulator mounting screws

∧

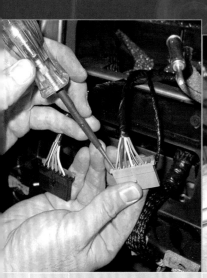

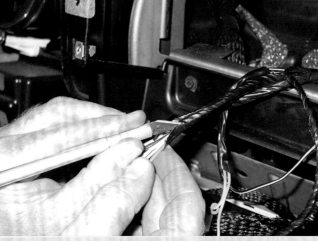

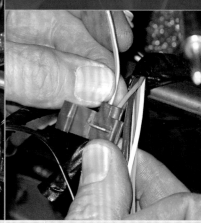

04 Follow the manufacturer's instructions for connecting the power wires for the FM modulator. Here we consulted the wiring diagram in our Haynes manual and found B+ power and accessory (switched) wires with a test light (this is at the head unit electrical connector)

05 If necessary, carefully cut back some of the wire harness tape to give yourself some working room

06 For convenience, the connections for the B+ power wire and accessory (switched) wire were made using Scotchlok connectors. Be sure to check that the connectors are compatible with the wire gauge sizes

07 Using electrical tape, secure the wires together for a neat and clean finish

08 Find a suitable place to connect the modulator unit earth wire to a good earthing point

09 At the back of the stereo head unit, follow the manufacturer's instructions and connect the vehicle's aerial cable to the modulator's aerial input, then connect the modulator output to the head unit's aerial input

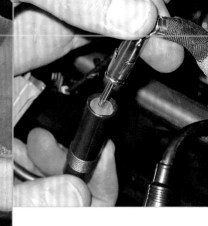

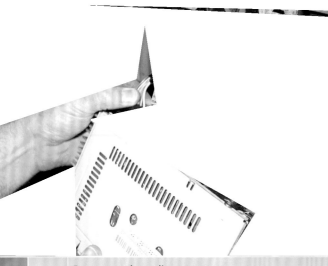

10 Reconnect the radio connectors . . .

11 . . . and mount the head unit back into the dash

12 Run the control wire to the changer's mounting location. We removed the sill plate . . .

16 . . . then drilled holes for the mounting bolts . . .

17 . . . and bolted the brackets in place. Notice how we reinforced the back of the panel with a thin board to make for a secure mount

18 Be sure to adjust the changer's horizontal/vertical screws (if equipped) to the proper setting

19 After installing the trim panel and changer, the control cable can be connected

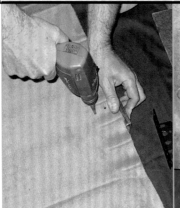

13 . . . and placed the cable under the carpet

14 We're going to mount the changer to the trim panel behind the seat

15 After removing the panel we marked where the mounting brackets needed to be placed . . .

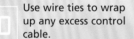

20 Use wire ties to wrap up any excess control cable.

21 Route the control unit and cable from the FM modulator to a convenient location. With the installation complete, follow the manufacturer's instructions, tuning the head unit to the proper FM station, then test the player.

22 Our final task was to mount the controller; we accomplished this by using Velcro and attached it to the centre console

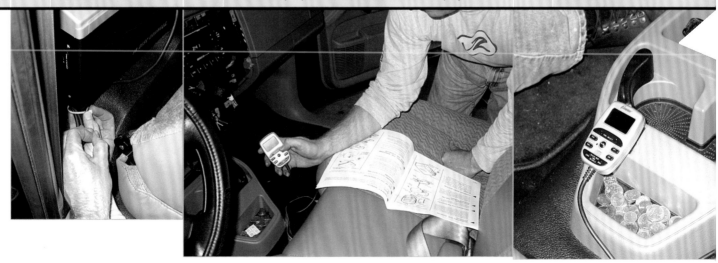

Mobile Video

It's not just about cranking up the jams. Mobile video systems are available so you can watch DVDs, hook up TV, video tape players or even video game consoles. We spend a lot of time in our rides. So why not take your driving machine to the next level?

What was once an extravagance that would only be found in a limo, many mobile video system components are available to entertain passengers or impress your friends when just hanging out.

The simplest mobile video systems are portable, self-contained units which can be strapped into place between the two front seats. There are other systems similar to these, but they're built into the centre console and aren't easily removed like the portable type.

If this type of video system is not what you had in mind, a component system is your alternative. Basically a component system consists of a source, monitor and audio. With a component system, you have the flexibility to add monitors or different source units and create a custom, almost "theatre-like" environment.

1

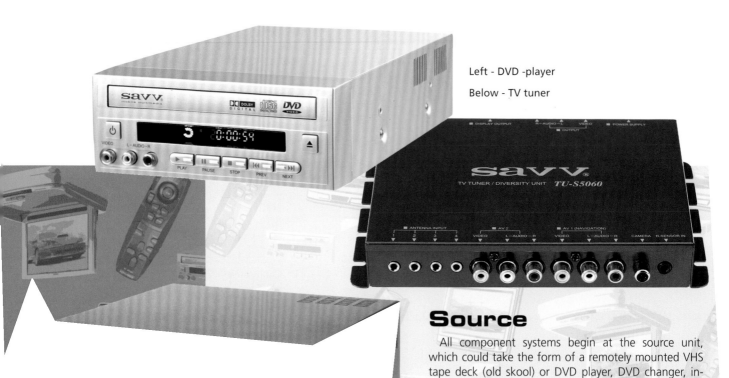

Left - DVD -player

Below - TV tuner

Source

All component systems begin at the source unit, which could take the form of a remotely mounted VHS tape deck (old skool) or DVD player, DVD changer, in-dash DVD player, in-dash multimedia player, an overhead flip-down screen with an integral DVD player, a game console, a TV tuner or a combination of these.

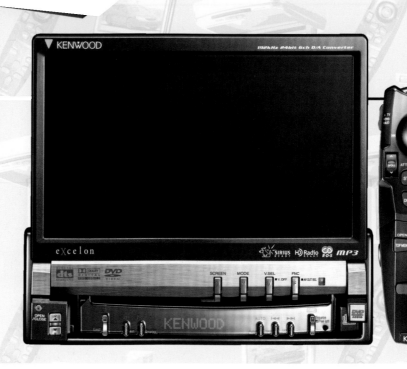

This in-dash DVD player features a motorised monitor that retracts when not in use. It is also an AM/FM radio receiver and TV tuner, plays CDs and MP3 format CDs

Overhead monitor

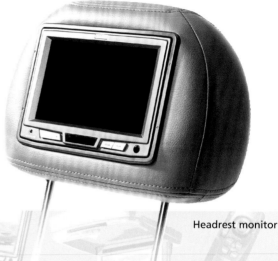

Headrest monitor

Switcher

Monitors

Monitor types include the in-dash motorised screen, sunvisor monitors, headrest monitors, flip-down overhead console monitors, centre console monitors, and monitors that can be mounted on a pedestal or bracket just about anywhere in the vehicle where there's enough room. Just keep in mind that no screen visible to the driver can be operational when the vehicle is in motion.

Sound

An option that's available with some systems are infrared headphones that allow passengers to listen to the movie or game audio track without the hassle of cords that could get in the way. The infrared signal on these systems is broadcast from transmitters embedded in the monitor housings or from a remote transmitter, usually mounted on the headlining or at the rear of the overhead console where the line-of-sight between the transmitter and headphone will be uninterrupted.

Audio can also be piped through the vehicle's existing speakers. If you've upgraded your audio system with a surround sound system, your passengers will be able to enjoy a near-theatre experience. The source unit can either be hard-wired into the system or an FM modulator can be used, which really simplifies the installation process.

Some inverters can plug into the cigarette lighter, but if you frequently use it for other items, consider hard-wiring it into the vehicle. Follow the manufacturer's instructions for wiring it. This inverter was installed under the back seat for connecting a video game console.

How can I connect my PlayStation 2 console?

Video game consoles can be integrated into the system by the use of a signal distribution box and a power inverter that converts 12 volts DC into 230 volts AC. And, with the use of a switchbox or video input jacks a video game console can be connected in no time at all.

The "what's legal and what's not" part . . .

Considering the issues of driver distraction involved with video monitors:

- An LCD panel and/or video monitor may be installed in a motor vehicle and visible to the driver if the LCD panel or video monitor is used for vehicle information, system control, rear or side observation or navigation.

- If the LCD panel or video monitor is used for television reception, video or DVD play, the LCD or video monitor must be installed so that these features will only function when the vehicle's handbrake is applied.

- An LCD panel or video monitor used for television reception, video or DVD play that operates when the vehicle is in gear or when the handbrake is not applied must be installed to the rear of the driver's seat where it will not be visible, directly or indirectly, to the operator of the motor vehicle.

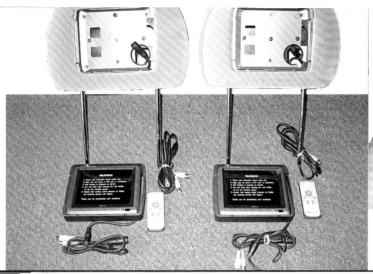

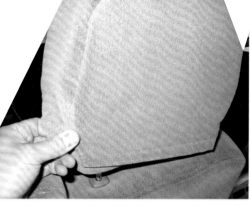

Purchasing an optional headrest cover is not only a good security measure, but it can also protect your monitor from dirt or scratches when not in use

Mobile video system installation
Vehicle-specific headrests

So you've decided to install headrest monitors, but cutting into the factory headrests, scooping out some foam, installing a frame then snapping the monitor into the frame is not what you had in mind. The easy option is installing vehicle-specific headrests. The installation requires no disfiguring headrest modification - the vehicle-specific headrests are designed to replace the factory headrests and after a few easy steps a monitor can be installed.

01 After removing the factory headrest, we started by unsnapping the fabric at the bottom of the seat back

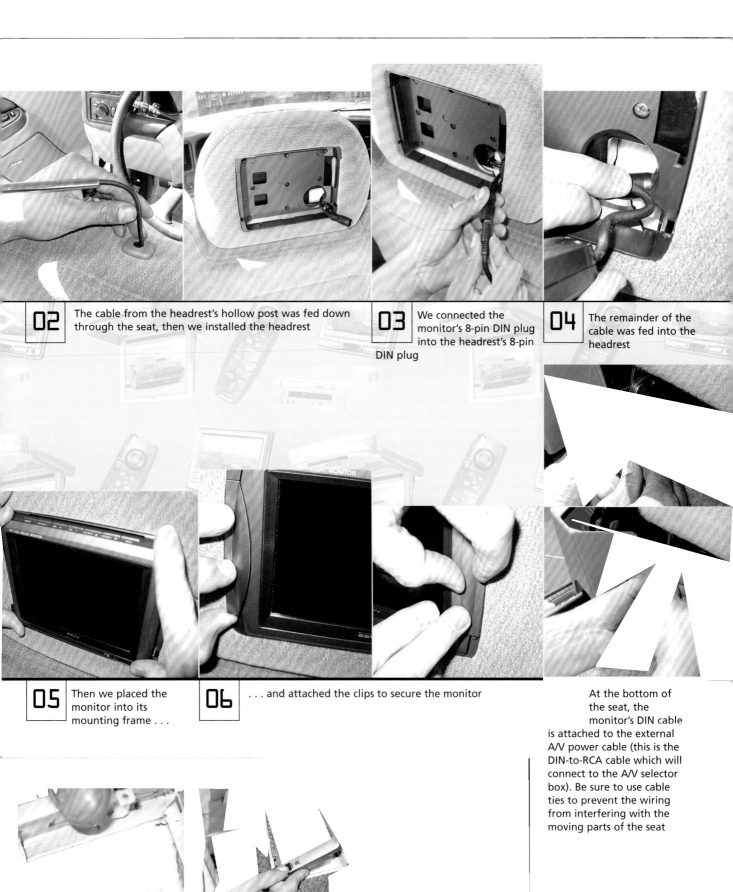

02 The cable from the headrest's hollow post was fed down through the seat, then we installed the headrest

03 We connected the monitor's 8-pin DIN plug into the headrest's 8-pin DIN plug

04 The remainder of the cable was fed into the headrest

05 Then we placed the monitor into its mounting frame . . .

06 . . . and attached the clips to secure the monitor

At the bottom of the seat, the monitor's DIN cable is attached to the external A/V power cable (this is the DIN-to-RCA cable which will connect to the A/V selector box). Be sure to use cable ties to prevent the wiring from interfering with the moving parts of the seat

Headrest monitor installation

If no vehicle-specific headrests with monitors are available for your vehicle, or for some reason you want to retain your headrests, you can modify them to accept video monitors. If you take your time and work carefully you will wind up with a very clean-looking installation, and save a little cash as well. The only real drawback to choosing this route is that the cable to the monitor will be slightly exposed if the headrest is raised.

01 Mark the fabric to be cut on the headrest, using the inside of the housing as a template. Be sure to centre the housing and make sure it's straight!

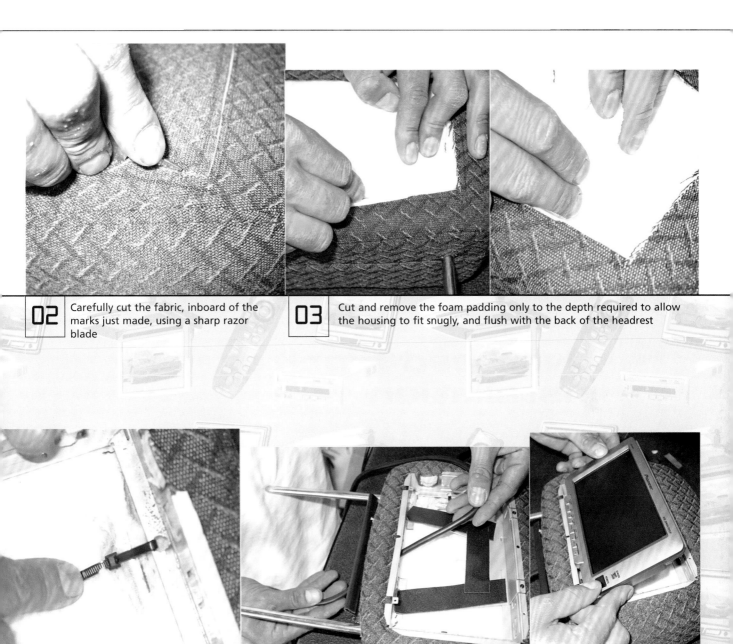

02 Carefully cut the fabric, inboard of the marks just made, using a sharp razor blade

03 Cut and remove the foam padding only to the depth required to allow the housing to fit snugly, and flush with the back of the headrest

04 Since headrest designs differ between manufacturers, you'll have to figure out a way to mount the housing. With this particular headrest we used a number of cable ties to hold the housing to the headrest support posts

05 The monitor's A/V wire should be fed through the housing then exit at the bottom of the headrest next to one of the support posts

06 Connect the A/V wire, then mount the monitor into the housing following the manufacturer's instructions

Overhead monitor installation

Too many kids? Not enough headrests? Install an overhead monitor and keep everyone happy!

Several overhead monitors are supplied with generic housings. The kit comes with everything needed to install an overhead monitor that looks almost factory.

01 Installing an overhead monitor requires dropping part of the vehicle's headlining

02 This overhead monitor is replacing the vehicle's courtesy light

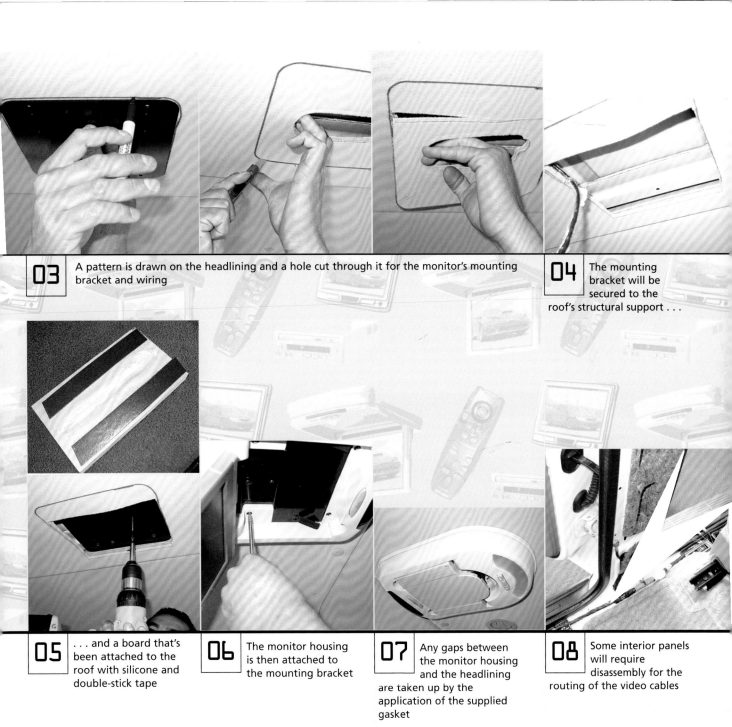

03 A pattern is drawn on the headlining and a hole cut through it for the monitor's mounting bracket and wiring

04 The mounting bracket will be secured to the roof's structural support . . .

05 . . . and a board that's been attached to the roof with silicone and double-stick tape

06 The monitor housing is then attached to the mounting bracket

07 Any gaps between the monitor housing and the headlining are taken up by the application of the supplied gasket

08 Some interior panels will require disassembly for the routing of the video cables

DVD player installation

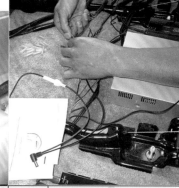

01 A stand-alone DVD player can be mounted in a convenient location like this under the middle seat

02 Using the supplied mounting brackets, the player can be secured to the floor in no time at all

03 Follow the manufacturer's instructions for connecting the power wires

04 A DVD player with accessory inputs, makes it possible to connect a video game console or an alternative video source

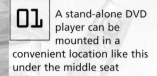

??? FAQs

Mobile video

If I want to install headrest monitors, do I need to cut up my headrests?
Vehicle specific headrests are available for most vehicles, making it unnecessary to cut the factory headrests.

How many speakers will I need for multi-channel surround sound?
Four side speakers, two in front and two in the rear. Also you'll need a centre speaker and a subwoofer.

How much information can be stored on a DVD disc?
A single-sided DVD can hold up to 4.7GB.

If I purchase a DVD player, will the player also play my CDs?
Most DVD players can play back audio CD's as well.

05 If the DVD player has a remote sensor, mounting it somewhere on the dash is a smart choice

I have two sets of headphones for my video system but they are always getting tangled or tripped over. What can I do?
Wireless headphone systems are available that transmit the audio signal using either infrared or radio frequency transmitters.

Is it possible to integrate my video system's audio with my vehicle's factory audio system?
Yes, the easiest solution would be to use an FM modulator but if you want to upgrade, replace the factory head unit with a DVD player or multimedia station.

What type of video system is the easiest to install?
The portable, self-contained units are probably the easiest for the do-it-yourselfers. Installing them is usually a matter of connecting the power wire to the 12-volt power outlet (cigarette lighter).

What size monitors?
For now, monitors for a vehicle range in size from 5 to 20 inches.

3 input - 3 output video selector installation

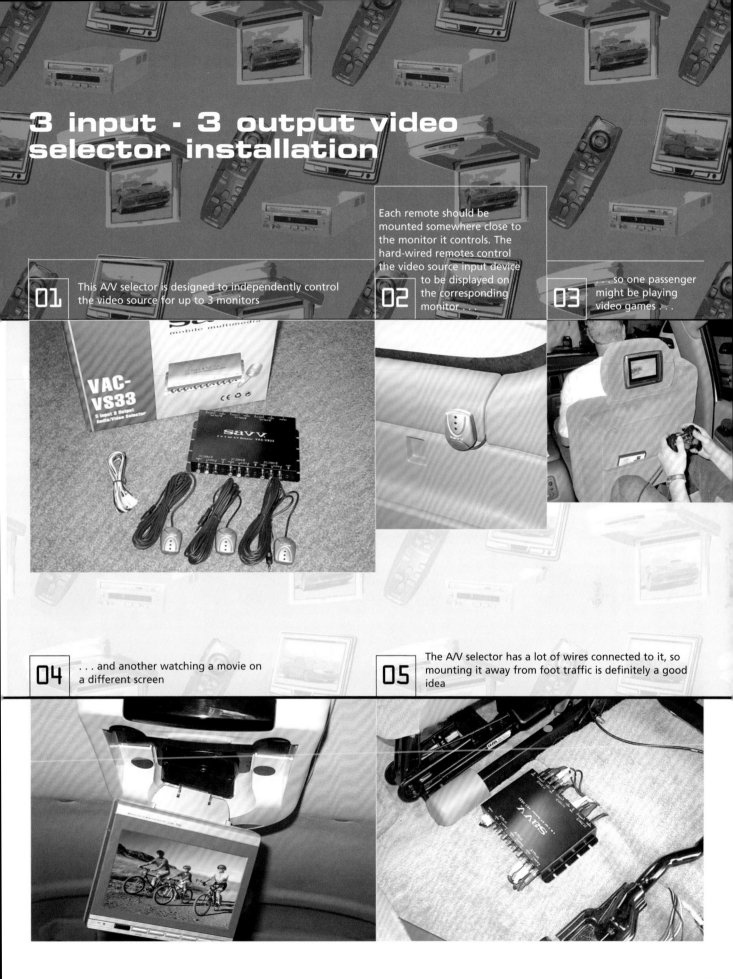

01 This A/V selector is designed to independently control the video source for up to 3 monitors

02 Each remote should be mounted somewhere close to the monitor it controls. The hard-wired remotes control the video source input device to be displayed on the corresponding monitor . . .

03 . . . so one passenger might be playing video games . . .

04 . . . and another watching a movie on a different screen

05 The A/V selector has a lot of wires connected to it, so mounting it away from foot traffic is definitely a good idea

screen

Bored of your CDs? Nothing on the radio? We have just the thing if you and a mate get bored, stuck in a 10-mile tailback on a bank holiday. Definitely a growing trend on the ICE scene, no top modded motor's complete these days without a games console, screen, DVD - where d'you stop? Just don't get caught playing it while you're moving, that's all.

01 Won't see much without a screen, so let's do that first. The trickiest bit of all is deciding where it'll go - obviously, both front seat people have to see it, so somewhere central, but how high up? Try the screen and its bracket in place, and check it adjusts how you want it. Is it accessible from below/behind, for feeding-in the wires? We chose this spot next to the centre vents.

02 Removing one of those vents would obviously make fitting the screen much easier, so not being afraid to pull things apart, we did. Once the glovebox was out of the way (see how we fitted the auxiliary fusebox in 'Accessories and necessities'), the vent could be 'helped' out from inside.

03 This is the mounting plate for the screen - hold this in place, and mark for drilling a hole. As this goes right into your lovely dash, check you've got it right a few times . . .

04 . . . before getting the drill out. I think this is what they call the point of no return.

05 That hole also has to be big enough to take the screen's video lead, and its plug, which is quite chunky. It's likely you'll have to supersize it with a file. Although the dash is pretty solid, it makes sense to brace the mounting using a large ('panel') washer on the inside.

06 Fit the screen to the mounting bracket, then feed in the video lead and the plug. Using our large washer and the nut provided, making the screen a solid fit on the dash wasn't hard . . .

. . . and with the new headset not yet fitted, neither was feeding up the other half of the video lead, for connection behind the dash. This Centurion screen's a budget model, but still has built-in speakers and even a headphone socket. Looks good, but it's not working yet - let's finish the job.

Our screen came with an all-in-one lead containing the three-part video feed from the X-Box (or PS2/DVD), and also the power supply/earth. We'll connect up the X-Box later - for now, we want power to our screen. They give you a cigar lighter plug, but this looks a bit pants - let's wire it in properly. Chop the plug off, strip the ends, and we have skinny red and black wires.

The red's a live feed (you guessed it), which we're taking from our auxiliary fusebox (fitted in the 'Accessories and necessities' section).

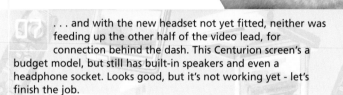

10 Finding an earth point for the black wire's not difficult either. Down in the driver's footwell, we drilled us a hole in the metal bodywork (mind those other wires) . . .

11 . . . then fitted a nut and bolt through, and we've got all the earth we can handle.

12 Connect the power plug in the screen's all-in-one lead, and the little green lights now tell us the screen's ready for input - let's give it some.

X-Box

To give power to your console, you need an AC inverter - ours was about £50 from Comet. What this does is take your car's 12-volt DC electrics, and turns it into mains voltage, giving you a domestic three-pin socket in your car - how cool is that? As with our screen, our inverter came with a fag lighter plug, which we dismantled. The wire we're snipping here is the earth . . .

01

. . . which we attached a ring terminal to, and bolted to an earth point we made at the back of the boot.

02

We stripped the end of the live wire, soldered it to one of the live feeds we were using for one of the amps . . .

03

. . . and then refitted it to our boot-mounted distribution block.

04

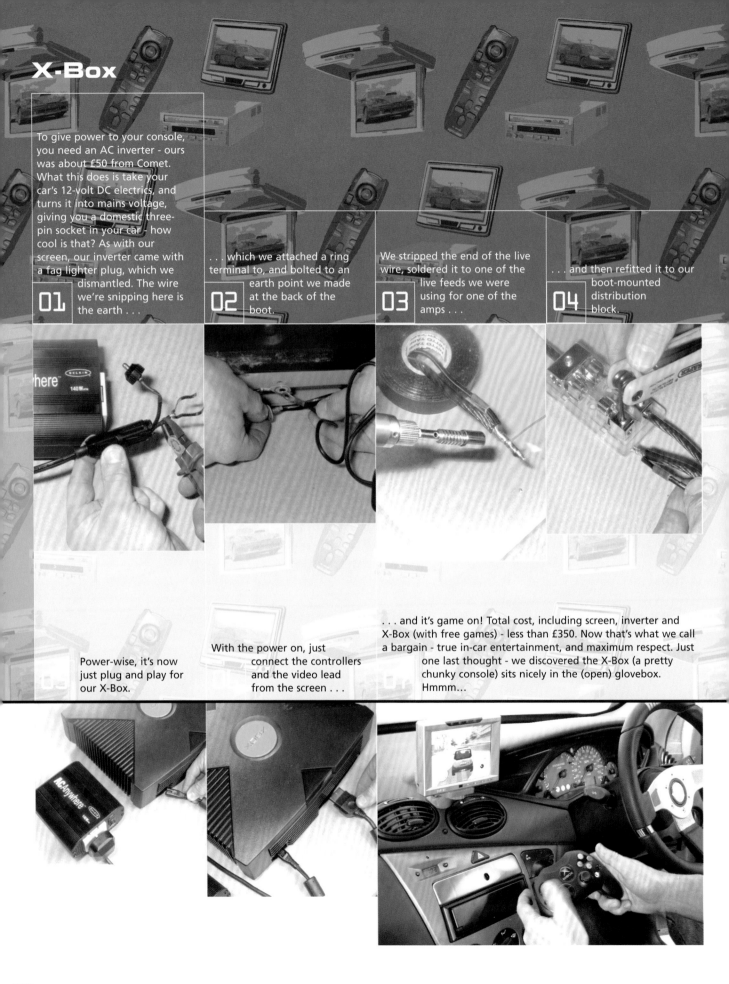

Power-wise, it's now just plug and play for our X-Box.

With the power on, just connect the controllers and the video lead from the screen . . .

. . . and it's game on! Total cost, including screen, inverter and X-Box (with free games) - less than £350. Now that's what we call a bargain - true in-car entertainment, and maximum respect. Just one last thought - we discovered the X-Box (a pretty chunky console) sits nicely in the (open) glovebox. Hmmm...

Playstation

Like the X-Box on page 108, the Playstation needs an AC inverter to turn the car's DC power into mains AC. As with our screen, our inverter came with a fag lighter plug, which we dismantled. This time, we took the live feed and earth

01 from the same places as our amplifier (heavier leads).

Our inverter had to be in the boot, to be near the PS2 itself - but we didn't want to make a feature of it. There was a handy gap between our sub box and amp (which would later be covered over by a false floor), so we mounted our inverter onto the box. We struggled a bit for some kind

02 of mounting bracket, but we managed to make one from a huge Jubilee clip . . .

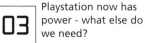

. . . and there he is, wired-up and looking sweet. The Playstation now has

03 power - what else do we need?

There's a whole bunch of wires to run down the car, so this is a good excuse to remove a seat or two and lift the carpets (if you want to do a neat job, that is). Besides the two controllers, there's the video/ audio outputs to our screen to connect. Luckily, they're so

04 well colour-coded, there's no danger of messing this up.

Just to ensure nothing goes wrong when those carpets go back down, tape up each connection. This stops them coming apart, and also stops

05 the connectors earthing-out on the car floor.

With power and video leads connected, and a screen that's ready to go, choose a suitable

06 secure spot for the console, and it's plug . . .

. . . and play. Our first-ever Playstation install, and it goes like a

07 dream. Total cost, including screen, inverter and PS2 (with free game) - about £400. Now that's what we call a bargain - true in-car entertainment, and maximum respect.

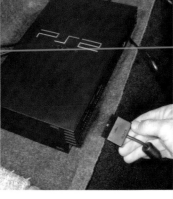

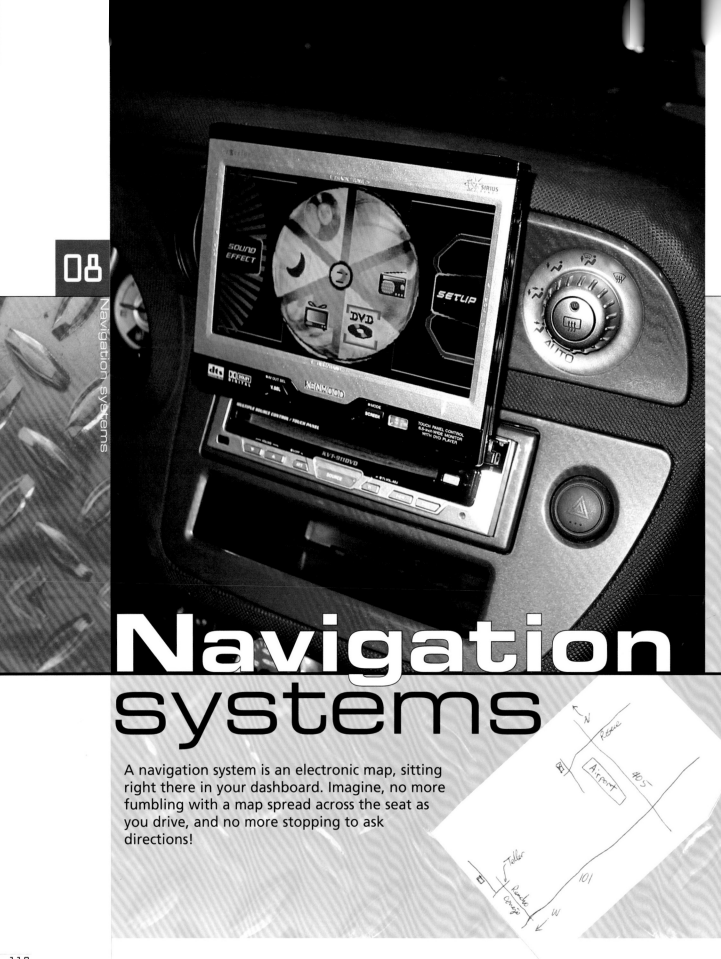

Navigation
systems

A navigation system is an electronic map, sitting right there in your dashboard. Imagine, no more fumbling with a map spread across the seat as you drive, and no more stopping to ask directions!

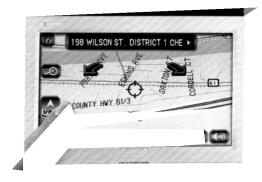

Voice activated

The first voice activated navigation systems reached the market in the mid-'90s. A voice activated system operates via a specially designed CD-ROM or DVD that contains a database of roads, motorways, landmarks and thousands of points of interest (POI). Each street name, road, city and POI has been recorded on the CD-ROM or DVD, which is loaded into a specially designed changer or player. The user can activate the system via microphone mounted in the car by saying a specific word like, "Navigator." The voice activated system then asks a series of questions like "Where are you starting from?" or "Where do you want to go?" The system then gives you verbal commands, telling you where and when to turn, guiding you effortlessly to your destination.

Telepath™

This system was developed by Delco Electronics (a division of General Motors). Telepath uses the Global Positioning Satellite (GPS) signal to calculate its current location. It also employs a dead-reckoning system that uses a compass and the vehicle speed sensor to calculate the position of the vehicle just in case GPS signals aren't detectable.

The user inputs the destination via a small LCD type display. Destinations can be entered via address, intersection, or landmark (such as "ATM" or "PETROL"). The information database is contained on a flash-memory card. The system directs the driver with an arrow and shows the distance to the destination.

Presently, there are four basic navigation systems in the global marketplace:

1 Voice activated.
2 Telepath™.
3 GPS (Global Positioning Satellite) locators.
4 Advanced Route Guidance systems.

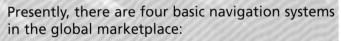

~~G~~PS locators

GPS locator systems utilise a *"moving map"* on a video screen in the vehicle to direct the driver. This system utilises a digitised map of a specific area with "hidden" longitude and latitude coordinates. The system incorporates a GPS receiver. The GPS receiver must receive at least three GPS satellite signals to determine the correct longitude and latitude coordinates. The GPS information is then compared to the digitised map data. When the current location is found on the map, that image of the map is displayed on the screen.

These systems rely only on the GPS signal to find the location of the vehicle. This system *does not* take into account vehicle speed or direction, therefore, turn-by-turn guidance is sometimes not completely accurate. This system can show the driver the destination on the digitised map, but it's up to the driver to figure out how to get from Point A to Point B. Many of these types of systems are also portable, enabling the driver to remove the unit and proceed on foot, if necessary.

Advanced route guidance systems

This type of system utilises three different input sensors to determine the present location and track the progress of the vehicle:

GPS aerial/receiver - uses GPS satellites to determine the current position of the vehicle.

Gyro sensor - determines the direction in which the vehicle turns.

Vehicle Speed Sensor (VSS) - determines how far and how fast the vehicle has travelled.

Thanks to the gyro sensor and speed sensor, these systems more accurately display the vehicle's position and track the vehicle's progress - even when driving in areas where the GPS signal may be blocked.

Here are the basic elements of an advanced route guidance navigation system:

Main navigation ECU - the "brains" of the navigation system. Includes a built-in gyroscopic sensor, speed pulse sensor, Global Positioning Satellite receiver, and DVD or CD-ROM drive. It processes:
- The incoming data from the vehicle's speed sensor.
- The speed of the vehicle.
- The direction coming from the gyro sensor.

GPS aerial - receives incoming satellite signals.
- The aerial has a small footprint and some have a magnetic base.
- It's designed to be mounted with inside applications as well as outside of the vehicle.
- The aerial must have a clear view to the sky to receive satellite information.
- GPS reception can be slightly reduced when the aerial is mounted inside the vehicle.

CD-ROMs or DVDs - contain the maps for each locale (which can be updated periodically).
- Some companies rely on universal mapping software.
- Other companies provide customised DVD or CD-ROM discs.
- DVD has the ability to store entire countries.
- On some systems, when you install the system, you have to install the correct CD for your geographic area. Other systems allow you to swap CDs when you change geographic areas.

Video monitor - displays directions.
- Some monitors include a built-in speaker.
- Some monitors can be used to interface and control the audio system.
- Most monitors allow the driver to "zoom in" and "zoom out" to show more or less detail on the map.

Remote control - many systems include a wireless remote control to help operate the navigation system.

What's it going to cost me?

Knowing exactly where you are can put a serious dent in your pocket book! So shop around and decide what system is for you.

Basics of installation

There are countless ways to install a navigation system. Accordingly, we do not have the luxury of being able to cover each application. Therefore, we will cover the basics. Following are the basic guidelines you should follow when installing an Advanced Route Guidance navigation system.

Mounting the ECU

On some systems, the main navigation computer is designed to be mounted in the boot; on others, it can be mounted in the boot or the glove box (depending on the available space). It must be mounted in a location free of moisture or extreme heat, and it must be mounted horizontal (less than 5°), the gyro sensor mounted inside the ECU will not work properly when the unit is mounted on its side.

Mounting the aerial

The GPS aerial needs to be mounted in a location that is the most "visible" to the GPS satellites. Therefore, you need to carefully plan the location. When determining the mounting location, follow these guidelines:

- Do not mount under any metal surface.
- Some window tinting material has a high metal content (titanium), which can reduce the GPS aerial's reception.
- Some vehicles incorporate special heat-resistant glass that will cause GPS reception problems. For these situations, it's best to install the GPS aerial on the roof or the boot lid.
- Mounting the aerial under dense plastics or cardboard may inhibit reception.
- The GPS aerial can receive the needed signals when mounted inside the vehicle, but some precautions must be taken to ensure proper performance. Mount the aerial in a location in the vehicle that allows the best "line-of-sight" performance. Locations such as the rear parcel shelf or front dash work the best.
- Secure the aerial with double-sided tape or silicone (this helps prevent the magnetic base from moving and scratching the paint).
- Carefully route the aerial cable and connect it to the ECU.
- The antenna is matched to its cable length - do not shorten or extend it.
- Avoid making sharp bends in the cable.
- Wind excess cable into large loops and secure with cable ties.

Mounting the monitor

Like most installations, you have to plan out where you want to install the monitor. It needs to be convenient, yet unobtrusive - you don't want it blocking any of the vital controls. Try to mount the monitor so it can be seen without too much distraction. If the monitor will be mounted low, angle it up for best performance. Don't mount the monitor where it could be struck by an airbag in the event of an accident. Also, most monitors come with a fixed length of cable that cannot be extended. Keep this in mind when routing the monitor cable to the ECU.

Once the installation is complete, adjust the monitor's brightness level for best performance. Most monitors have a separate brightness adjustment for day and night viewing (when you turn on the side lights, the display dims).

Wiring

Wiring most navigation systems is about as simple as wiring a CD changer or a head unit. Typically, there are only six wires to connect on the main harness. If there are any remaining wires, they are usually used to connect the navigation system to the audio system.

FAQs Navigation

How does a navigation system determine my position and track my progress?

On most systems this information is determined by basically three things: The GPS aerial/receiver, gyro sensor and the Vehicle Speed Sensor. These systems accurately display the vehicle's position and track the vehicle's progress - even when driving in areas where the GPS signal may be blocked.

What can a navigation system do for me?

A good navigation system can give you step-by-step directions to your programmed destination as you're driving.

Where is the best place to mount my GPS aerial?

Inside or outside the vehicle. Mounting the aerial inside the vehicle may prove to be more a difficult mounting location as the aerial cannot receive signals through metal. Follow the manufacturers instructions.

Why do I need to connect my navigation system to my Vehicle Speed Sensor?

Some navigation systems use the Vehicle Speed Sensor information to track the vehicle's speed and travel distance. This information, along with the information received from the navigation unit's built-in gyroscopic sensor, help to more accurately display the vehicle's position and track its progress.

Can a GPS system track where my car is or has been?

Yes, tracking systems are now available to anyone who wants to track a vehicle, even families who want to keep track of their teenage drivers.

Navigation systems

Big Brother in a Box

Speed cameras have to be one of the most unpopular things ever. We're talking worse than exams, dentists, alcohol-free beer, and the Budget. Does anyone actually like them? Well, the makers do - they should all be living it up on a beach in the Bahamas. The people making speed camera signs are obviously lovin' it. And the Chancellor? Nuff said.

Speed, of course, is fun. The sensation of speed is the main reason we enjoy driving, and it's one of the best ways to show off your motor. There's nothing like giving your ride a good caning, being pushed back in the seat, exhaust snarling, engine singing. Sounds like fun to me - so these things are really fun cameras, then?

Like it or not, we live in a world obsessed with limiting speed. Excess speed, we're told, causes accidents and costs lives. As most of us have realised by now, excess speed really means more money for the Government. What causes accidents is driving like a tw*t. But they don't have cameras for that.

Before we get ourselves in too much trouble, we have to admit the cameras might save lives in built-up areas with lots of peds, kids and old folk about. Driving like a hooligan in those situations probably should get you a slap on the wrist for 'endangering lives'. But at night, on a dead-straight road with no traffic? We think not.

Pay attention

The best you can say about cameras is that they're a necessary evil which we all have to live with. So what's the best way of avoiding the 'bad news' letter in the post?

There is one 100% foolproof method, which is totally legal, and it's dead simple - don't ever speed. That should do the trick. Yeah, right. Back in the real world, everyone speeds some time, even if it's only by a few mph. Add a few more miles-per because you weren't really watching your speed, and then do it somewhere there's a camera (or a sneaky mobile trap you'd never spotted before), and you're nicked. Is it any wonder that clean licences are getting as rare as rocking-horse leftovers?

Even on roads you know well, the do-gooders are forever lowering the limits, so if you don't watch it, you'll be sailing through more than 10 mph over today's new limit. And that's definitely worth a few points! You've gotta concentrate, to stay clean.

Know your enemy

First of all, you've got to know what you're up against. It's the only way (short of the fantasy world of never, ever speeding) that you stand a chance. And the first thing to know is - not all cameras are the same. Some can even be beaten.

Gatso (and PEEK)

The first, the best-known, the most common, and probably the most-hated. Invented by the winner of the 1953 Monte Carlo Rally, Gatsos are the familiar large, square box in stealth grey or high-viz yellow, with a square lens and flash unit (the later, less-common PEEK cameras have two round items, set one above the other). These are radar-operated (type 24) and can only 'get' you from behind, because they use a flash to take the photo, and this would blind you if it went off with you coming towards it. These cameras, therefore, cannot in theory catch you speeding towards them (don't quote us on that). As a result of this limitation, some authorities will turn the cameras round from time to time, to catch you out.

RLCs are also Gatso-based, but they work through sensors in the road, which are active when the lights are on red. If your car passes over them in this condition, it's gotcha. Some RLCs use radar too, so if you speed through on red, you'll also get a speeding fine. Gee, thanks.

Truvelo

Oooh, nasty. The forward-facing 'gatso' is particularly unpleasant, but luckily for us, it's also more expensive than the rear-facing Gatso, so not as common. Yet. The Truvelo camera can be recognised by two round lenses side by side in the centre of its box, and one of these is a pinky-red colour (hence the 'pinkeye' nickname). The unusual pink 'lens' is actually a flash unit, fitted with a red filter to avoid blinding the driver. Because the photo's taken from the front, it's hard for the driver to claim someone else was driving, or that they 'don't know'

Gatsos have 35 mm film inside, with about 400 shots possible before the film runs out. It's obviously vital that the film is recovered from the camera, or a prosecution can't be made - these cameras get vandalised for all sorts of reasons. Some cameras are rumoured not to contain any film, so they flash without recording any evidence (that bloke down the pub could be wrong, though).

If the radar detects excess speed, the flash is triggered twice as you pass over the measured line markings on the road. From the distance you travel between the set flashes, your speed can be proved. It's anyone's guess where the trigger speed for a camera will be set, but it's almost bound to be quite a few mph over the posted limit - if it wasn't, the camera would quickly catch dozens of speeders, and run out of film. Be more wary of inner-city Gatsos, as they're probably 'emptied' more often, allowing a lower speed tolerance.

tricks 'n' tips
In a thirty limit, you're less likely to speed if you hook a lower gear than normal. Most cars will comfortably cruise through a thirty in 4th gear, but it's too easy to add speed in 4th. Try using 3rd, and the natural engine braking (and extra engine/exhaust noise) will help you keep a lid on your speed. It's not foolproof, but give it a try anyway.

who was driving (a common ploy to try and 'get off' Gatso offences). The less-visible flash gives less warning to following motorists, too. Not that we're suggesting they're out to get us. Oh no.

These babies are triggered by the car passing over piezo sensors set into the road, not radar. If you see three stripes across your path, slow the heck down.

Red Light Cameras

Intended to catch people who go through traffic lights on red. Which, you have to say, is pretty dodgy. And have you ever risked it on a single amber? If you remember your Highway Code, this means stop, the same as a red light. 'Amber-gamblers' should also beware the traffic-light cams, 'cos they'll get you one day. Unlike (a few) points for speeding, points for traffic light offences will really hurt your insurance premiums, so watch it.

SPECS

Yikes - this really is Big Bro stuff. This system uses digital cameras (no film needed), mounted high on special gantries - these are a set distance apart, and create a speed monitoring zone. When you 'enter the zone', your number plate is recorded digitally, with a date and time stamp (regardless of whether you're speeding). When you leave the zone, another camera does the same thing. Because you've travelled a known distance between the two cameras, it's possible to calculate your average speed - if you're over the limit for the stretch of road, the computer spits out a fine in your direction.

What's really worrying about this technology is that it can be used to cross-check you and your car for other offences (whether your car's taxed and MoT'd, for instance). Anything dodgy, and the next time you pass by those cameras at that time of day, you could be in for a jam-sandwich surprise. Still, it could also catch the crims making off with your motor…

Mobile or temporary speed traps

These are either Gatso, Mini-Gatso, or laser type.

The potential Gatso sites are easy enough to spot - look for three shiny strips across the road, with a sturdy grey metal post alongside, on the pavement. Mr Plod comes along, sets up his camera (which uses sensors in the road strips not radar to detect your speed), catches his daily quota of speeders, and moves on. Don't give him a short day by being one of his victims.

Mini-Gatsos are just smaller, mobile versions of the UK's least-favourite roadside 'furniture', operated out of cop-cars and anonymous white vans - to get you, you have to be driving away from them.

More sinister (and much on the increase) are the laser cameras, which are aimed at your number plate (usually the front one) and record your speed on video. Often seen mounted on tripods, on bridges overlooking busy roads, or hidden inside those white 'safety camera partnership' vans. Lasers have quite a range (1000 metres, or over half a mile), so by the time you've spotted them, they've spotted you speeding. It's up to the operator to target likely speeding vehicles - so will they pick on your maxed motor? You bet!

Beating the system

No-one's condoning regular speeding, but these days, it's just too easy to get 'done' for a fairly minor speed infringement. Which hardly seems fair. There must be some way of fighting back, surely?

Cheap and legal

Don't. Ever. Speed. Simple, but not easy in the real world. Next!

Neither cheap nor legal

The James Bond option

One of 007's older cars had self-changing number plates - this may have been the inspiration for a highly-illegal speed camera dodge. Since all the detection systems rely heavily on your number plate, some skankers drive round with false plates - they might even have copied yours. Worth remembering if you ever get accused of speeding in the Outer Hebrides. Getting caught on false plates could be a £1000 fine, so is it worth the risk?

For ages now, companies have been advertising 'photo-reflective' plates (they're not illegal, but the dibble take a dim view). Most are a rip-off, but some do appear to work – on traps which flash. Speed cameras take very high-res pictures, however - even if your plates don't give you away, the coppers might i.d. your motor from its non-standard features. Money wasted, then.

Cloaking device?

The mobile laser speed trap is one of the most common, and most hated, in the UK. It sends out a laser beam which targets your front number plate. Wouldn't it be great if you could buy something to mess up its signal, so it couldn't 'lock on' ? You can - it's called a laser diffuser (sometimes marketed under the guise of a remote garage door-opener). And yes, they do work - but careful fitting is needed, and the lenses need regular cleaning. If you're caught using it for speed trap evasion, you can be done for obstruction, or perverting the course of justice - it pays to have a well-placed 'off' switch.

Gatso-beating radar 'scramblers' are said not to work, while radar jammers are an illegal transmitter - using one could see you inside for much longer than a speeding conviction.

A sound investment?

Laser detectors

The makers say this is essential kit to combat the roaming camera van threat, but be careful. We said earlier that laser cams have a range of up to 1000 metres, but most operators don't trigger theirs until you're much, much closer than that. Which means you have far less time to react. As long as you're not the first car along, your laser detector may pick up laser 'scatter' from cars in front, but there isn't much scatter with a laser. It's said that some laser detectors will only go off if your car's already been targeted - and of course, it's too late by then.

Radar detectors

These have been around for ages, and started life in the US. They're good for detecting radar-based speed cameras (most Gatsos), and any old police radar guns still in use, but that's all. Don't buy an old one (you'll get lots of false alerts if it's not meant for Euro/UK use), or a cheap one (it might not have enough range to give you a chance). *Stop press: Looks like laser and radar detectors are finally going to be made illegal later this year (2004) — only GPS systems will be legal after this.*

GPS systems

Using Global Positioning Satellite technology, these devices are really speed camera site locators, not detectors. Using an onboard database of camera locations, they constantly monitor your car's position, and warn when you're approaching a 'danger area'. Providing you keep your dash-mounted podule updated (by downloading the latest camera/blackspot info from the maker's website), these will warn you of virtually every potential camera in the country, including Truvelo and SPECS. The only limitations are a lack of laser detection, and it won't get all the mobile sites.

You must download new info regularly, and this costs (you buy a subscription to the website). Also, if your system hasn't been in use for a while, it can take quite a few minutes for the pod to pick up the satellites it needs - during this time, you're unprotected. Don't buy secondhand units with no subscription left, as the makers sometimes can't (won't?) re-activate them.

A final word

Don't rely too heavily on even the best anti-camera technology - try and drive within the spirit, if not the letter, of the Law, with a detector as backup.

Road **Angel**

The most effective way to 'detect' a camera is to know where it is. Yeah – obviously! But with cameras still being hidden behind road signs and bridges, and increasing numbers of camera-kitted white vans, knowing where the cams are ain't easy.

A GPS locator monitors your car's position relative to known camera sites, and warns you when you're getting close. The latest offerings also warn when you're approaching schools and other areas where extra care is needed. These devices are definitely not illegal. They increase road safety, by telling you where 'accident blackspots' are – not when to brake…

tricks 'n' tips
Don't leave the mounting cradle fitted when you leave the car – it's all the clue a thief needs that there's some serious money's worth hidden in your glovebox. Even if it's not there (because you've sensibly taken it with you) you're still making it too tempting.

This latest Road Angel offers two main mounting options – a sticky-backed magnetic mount directly on the dash, or this rather neat screen-mounted cradle (also with a mag mount).

01 Either way, make sure the wipers don't obscure the unit's 'view', or the laser detection function won't stand a chance.

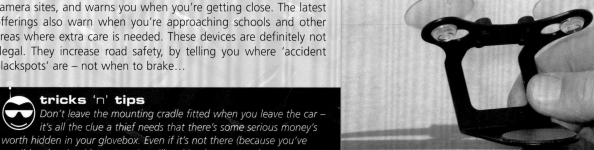

A GPS u…. only as good as the info it's working from – update it regularly by downloading the latest camera locations, or it's worse than useless. If you can use a PC well enough to download stuff from the Internet, you've got no worries.

Plug the unit into its lighter socket power supply (assuming it's not already taken by your phone charger or hands-free kit), then fit the unit to its bracket. First, you're greeted by a friendly message, then the unit starts searching for its satellites. While this is going on, remember that you're not protected.

Depending which system you've got, when you're getting near a camera site (sorry – accident blackspot), you'll get a warning beep or message, and the display will flash. If you miss all that lot, you probably need to downgrade your ICE install.

Accessories
and necessities

Before you can install head units, amplifiers, speakers or any other mobile electronic components, you still need to select the right wiring, connectors, fuses, circuit breakers, inverters (if necessary) and sound dampening materials. Without the right stuff, your system either won't work at all or it'll work, but won't sound as well as it could or last as long as it should. So study the sections in this chapter before you run out and buy stuff that turns out to be junk, or before you get so anxious to install your gear that you just start twisting and taping wires together. *Remember: Take your time and do it right!*

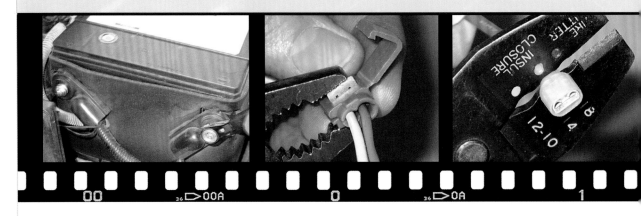

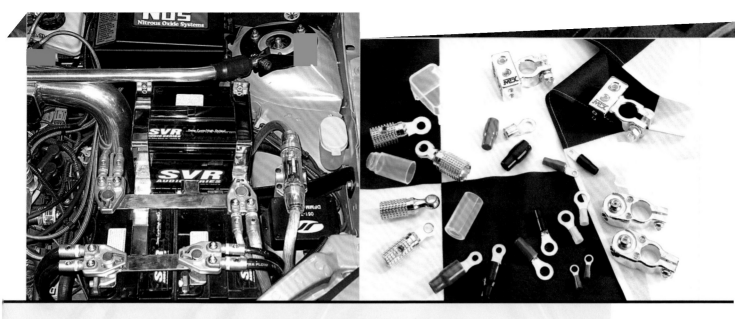

Battery connections:
it all begins, and ends, here

At the risk of overstating the obvious: A sound system is useless without the battery because that's where the power comes from. No one disputes this, nor does anyone deny that power-hungry amplifiers will suck all the current they can get from the battery. Yet the system's power and earth connections at the battery are often an afterthought, thrown together at the eleventh hour "just to get it running." Sure, you *intend* to get back to it . . . later, maybe (and you know what they say about the road to hell . . .). But, guess what? More often than not, later never arrives. Meanwhile, those funky battery connections that you threw together with some connectors you had laying around your garage slowly begin to get dirty and corroded. And the quality, or at least the peak power, of your sound system begins a long downhill slide.

Make no mistake. Skimp on the quality of the power and earth cables' battery terminal connectors and you'll end up with a six-month instead of a ten-year system. Poorly connected power wires at the battery can wreak havoc on an audio system. So keep your connections neat by replacing the battery cable clamps with aftermarket units that provide extra connections for cables or ring terminals.

Installing aftermarket battery cable connections

Start by disconnecting the cable from the negative battery terminal. *Always* disconnect the negative cable first! If you start by disconnecting the positive cable first, you run the risk of creating large and powerful sparks if the tool you are using to loosen the cable clamp comes into contact with a earth point on the vehicle (such as the body or other metal component). Not only can this burn you, it could also cause the battery to explode!

01

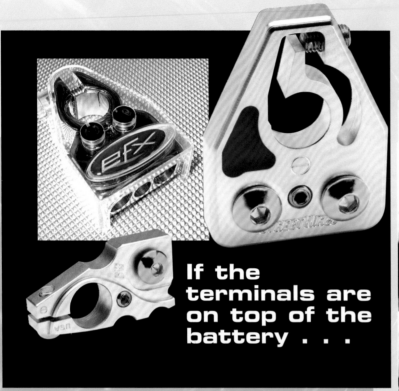

If the terminals are on top of the battery . . .

03 Clean the battery terminal posts with a battery terminal cleaning tool (available at most auto parts stores)

02 After you have disconnected the cable from the negative terminal, disconnect the cable from the positive terminal. Because they've been attached to the terminals for a long time, battery cables have some "memory" in them, which means they want to remain in the same position they're usually in, even when you disconnect them. So make sure that you not only set both cables aside but that you secure them in such a way so that they don't flop back into their connected positions and touch the battery terminals!

04 On some vehicles, you might need to cut off the battery cable clamps. If you do, make sure that you will have enough cable left to reach the terminal post. You don't want either battery cable so short that it's stretched tight when connected to its terminal

05 Strip off enough insulation from the battery cable so that when installed in the new terminal clamp, the part of the cable that's inside the terminal will be in full contact with the terminal. Make sure that the gauge of the cable matches the gauge of the hole in the clamp, then insert the exposed end of the cable into the terminal clamp and tighten it securely

06 Slide the new terminal clamp onto the battery post and tighten the pinch nut or bolt securely

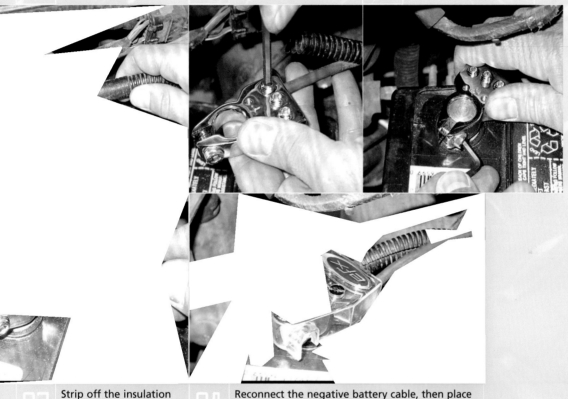

07 Strip off the insulation from the new amplifier power wire, make sure that the gauge of the power wire matches the gauge of the hole in the clamp, then insert the end of the wire into the new cable clamp and tighten the set screw securely

08 Reconnect the negative battery cable, then place the protective covers on the clamps. Transparent covers like the one shown here are not only good looking, they're practical too. They protect the terminal and clamp from dirt and moisture, and you can actually inspect the condition of the terminal and clamp without removing the cover

If the terminals are on the side of the battery . . .

If your vehicle's battery is equipped with side terminals, you'll need to add a side-mount adapter post to connect an audio power cable.

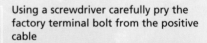

01 Start by disconnecting the cable from the negative battery terminal. Always disconnect the negative cable first! If you start by disconnecting the positive cable first, you run the risk of creating large and powerful sparks if the tool you are using to loosen the cable clamp comes into contact with a ground point on the vehicle (such as the body or other metal component). Not only can this burn you, it could also cause the battery to explode!

02 After you have disconnected the cable from the negative terminal, disconnect the cable from the positive terminal. Because they've been attached to the terminals for a long time, battery cables have some "memory" in them, which means they want to remain in the same position they're usually in, even when you disconnect them. So make sure that you not only set both cables aside but that you secure them in such a way so that they don't flop back into their connected positions and touch the battery terminals!

03 Using a screwdriver carefully pry the factory terminal bolt from the positive cable

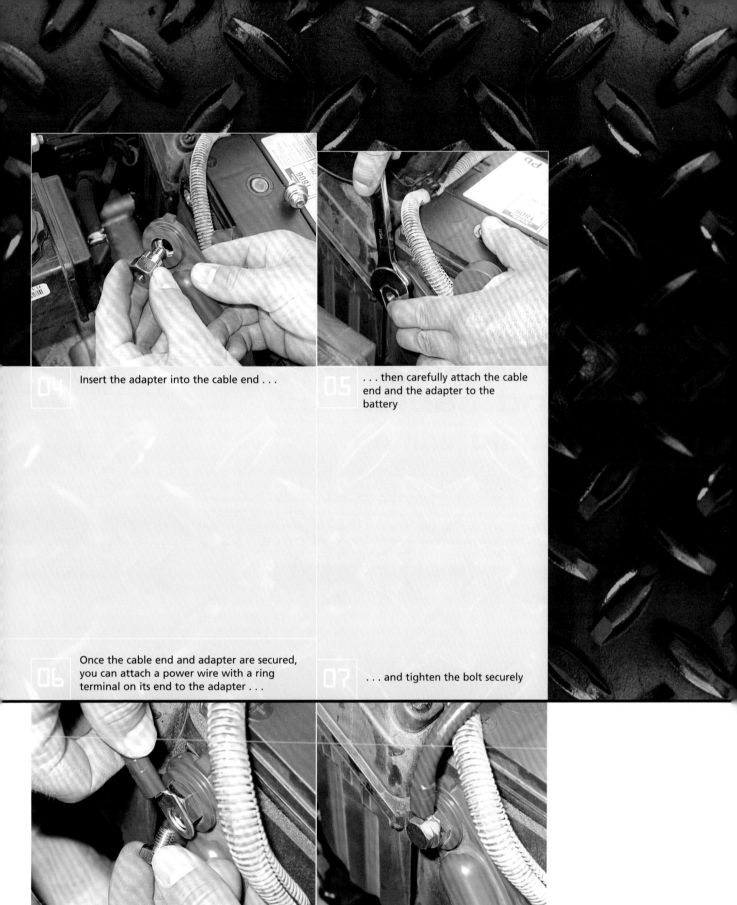

Insert the adapter into the cable end . . .

. . . then carefully attach the cable end and the adapter to the battery

Once the cable end and adapter are secured, you can attach a power wire with a ring terminal on its end to the adapter . . .

. . . and tighten the bolt securely

Electrical wiring and cables

Audio wiring

Until you've actually made a conscious effort to do your homework, it's difficult to appreciate the bewildering variety of special-purpose audio wiring available on the market today. The simplest wiring is constructed using one solid wire (known as single-strand wire) surrounded by some type of insulation, but this type of wire is rarely used in automotive audio installations. Like conventional wiring, audio wiring uses copper because it's the best conductor available for the money. (Silver and gold are better conductors, but way too expensive for most of us. Those for whom cost is no object occasionally use silver for very high-end audio applications. And connections are often gold-plated to provide corrosion resistance.) But copper wire is really the only similarity between audio and conventional wiring. Instead of a single strand of wire, audio wiring uses many strands or even bundles of strands. And it's often "shielded" to prevent interference from the signals in other nearby wires.

Resistance and skin effect

A couple of problems - resistance and "skin effect" - rear their ugly heads when audio or other types of mobile electronic components are wired together.

Skin effect is the rather racy name for a scientific phenomenon by which *electricity travels on the outside* (the "skin") *of a conductor.* Skin effect manifests itself in different ways depending on the application. In audio systems, it causes some distortion. Even in systems that use big gauge wires to reduce resistance, skin effect still causes some high-frequency distortion.

Now let's look at resistance, which is the opposition to the flow of current or an electrical signal in a wire. The resistance in a wire diminishes the strength of a signal as it travels through the wire. The longer the wire, the greater the amount of resistance. Resistance also causes some distortion. Single-strand wire has much higher resistance than stranded wire. If the diameter of a solid-conductor wire is too big, the signal is slightly distorted as a result of skin effect. If the diameter of the wire is too small, the resistance of the wire causes some distortion. These two phenomena overlap, so there is no perfect solution to the resistance-distortion problem regardless of which wire gauge you use.

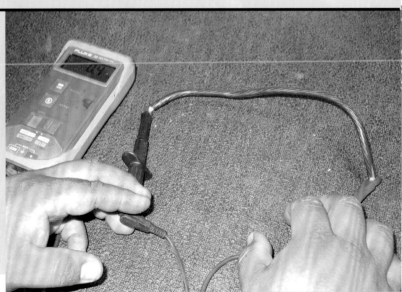

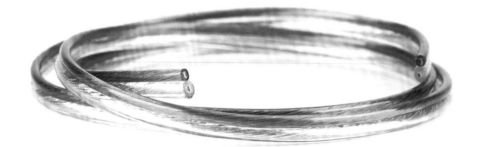

Stranded wires

Typical speaker wire consists of two stranded wires running parallel, and attached, to one another with some type of insulation covering them. Can you say massive resistance and skin effect? Audio cable manufacturers improved the performance of speaker cables by gradually twisting the wires throughout the length of the cable. Think of holding a bundle of wires (the strands) about two feet long with your hands at either end, then twisting the ends in opposite directions and you have the idea of twisted strands. The advantage of twisted strands is that each wire gradually moves from the centre to the outside of the strand, where most of the current travels. This technique significantly reduces the skin effect.

Some manufacturers also twist either stranded bundles or solid wires around an insulating core so that each of the wire strands within the bundle, or the surfaces of the single-strand wires is slowly turning, further mitigating the skin effect. And some manufacturers even insulate the bundles or solid wires, which keeps them at a certain distance from one another, preventing them from affecting one another.

Another type of audio cable consists of several twisted solid wires or stranded wire bundles arranged side by side in a parallel flat cable configuration. But the design, i.e. the twisted-strands, materials, etc. are the same as the cables described above.

Some general wiring guidelines

Decide where you're going to put each component

Before starting installation of a new sound system, first *decide where you are going to put each system component*. Then make a sketch of the entire system, including the components, the wiring and the connectors. Once you have made your own simple wiring schematic, it's much easier to sort out how and where you're going to route the electrical wires and cables connecting all these components. It also makes it easier to correctly estimate how much of each type of wire or speaker cable you'll need. And it will help you determine what types of connectors, and how many of each, you'll need.

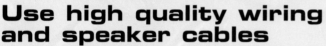

Use high quality wiring and speaker cables

When buying electrical wiring for power and signal cables, remember that poor system wiring can induce noise and cause overall poor performance, so don't skimp too much when it comes to your wiring. Cars generate some serious electromagnetic fields that mobile electronics systems can "receive" if their wiring uses cheap RCA (coaxial) cables with low quality shielding. Any time you mix low-power signal wires with high-power amps, you run the risk of accidentally creating an "aerial" that will "receive" this electromagnetically induced noise and feed it right into your amps and speakers. Typical symptoms include buzzing and whining noises as the engine revs rise and fall, or a ticking sound when you activate your turn signals. Low-quality cables and wires aren't the only source of this noise, but they are one variable over which you have some control. And good quality wires can simplify troubleshooting, because then you know that the wires themselves are not the problem.

Separate the power and signal cables

Always route power and signal cables so that they're physically separated. Power cables can induce noise in the low-power audio cables. The usual strategy for keeping them separated is to route the power cables along one side of the car and the low-power cables along the other side. If it's impossible to route the cables along the opposite sides of the floor, at least keep them separated by the transmission tunnel. Also, it's critical that you keep all low-power audio cables away from any other big electrical harnesses. Many modern vehicles already have a jungle of wiring underneath the carpeting. These wires bring battery voltage to all kinds of conveniences such as factory sound systems, power windows, central locking and power mirrors, rear taillights, etc. Even though they don't carry as much current as aftermarket sound systems, they have just as much voltage, and can induce noise in the system.

Keep your signal wires as short as possible

Keep your low-power signal wires (RCA or coaxial cables, usually) as short as possible. The longer they are, the more likely they are to act as an aerial that can receive noise from electromagnetic sources such as the engine ignition or the power amplifiers in your sound system. If you're going to buy pre-made cables with the connectors already attached to both ends, try to get cables that are long enough, but with very little extra length. In other words, if the choice is between two pre-made cables, one of which is too short and the other much too long, you're not going to buy a cable that's too short, but you don't want to buy a cable that's too long either. Walk away from both of those options and instead buy the correct length of uncut cable, then install your own connectors.

Earth loops and earth paths

Some professionals claim that 90 percent of all noise in a system can be traced back to incorrectly earthed components. When the components in a system aren't earthed correctly, they don't "see" exactly the same earth, which produces a phenomenon known as a "earth loop." This difference in the degree of being earthed is known as "earth potential." The difference in potential between all the earths of a system is what causes a earth loop, resulting in alternator whine.

There are several things you can do to prevent earths from developing into "loop" situations:

1) Use high-quality cable with good shielding for the low-power leads between the output of a head unit and the input of a crossover or amplifier. Inferior cable with poor shielding will allow noise to radiate into the system.
2) Never mount an amplifier or any other component to bare metal. Try to use an amp rack and then insulate all the other components from the vehicle chassis.
3) Don't earth several components to chassis earth through their earth lines. For example, some pre-amp units get their earth connection directly from the interconnect cable; connecting the black wire to earth on one of these units sets up an automatic earth loop. Also, if your pre-amps have a power supply earth that's separate from their signal earth, earth them to one point - usually the back of the radio.
4) Unless there's some kind of severe earthing problem with a vehicle, don't use aerial earth-breakers. The aerial earth is absolutely essential for AM reception.

The best strategy for avoiding these types of problems is to never share an earth connection with the vehicle's accessory earth path, such as a fan motor or a brake light earth. (If you do, you'll hear a pop or buzz whenever the fan is turned on or the brakes are applied!) Instead, earth everything through a single earth path to the negative side of the electrical system. In other words, connect the earth terminals for the head unit, the pre-amp(s), power amp(s), equaliser, crossover, etc. and then route one heavy-gauge earth wire to a point on the frame or unibody that will provide a resistance-free path back to the battery. And if you want to be really thorough, simply earth everything right to the battery itself.

Accessories and necessities

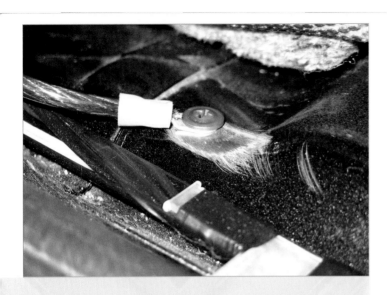

Finding a good earth

Try to avoid using earth points that are secondary body or chassis components (the bonnet, the boot lid, the doors, etc.). They might have tack welds or fasteners between the main and secondary body parts that produce higher resistance in the earth path back to the battery. Also try to avoid using earth points that share connections with other vehicle accessories. This will help you avoid potential noise problems.

Always avoid using the factory head unit power and earth wiring. The wire gauge is (usually) too small. And it often doesn't go directly to earth, but instead picks up the earths for other vehicle systems, all of which are gathered together at one earth point. Even though many standard head unit installation procedures specify a "factory harness adapter," systems with signal processors, multiple amplifiers and/or significant amounts of head unit power might be more prone to noise-related problems by using factory head unit wiring. This can produce clicks and pops in an audio system when other vehicle systems are switched on and off. Factory wiring also usually runs in harnesses that are located in close proximity to other electrical devices in the car that can radiate or couple noise into an audio system.

The best earth point on a vehicle is always some location *with a good physical connection to the same metal shared by the battery earth*. It doesn't necessarily have to be physically connected to the battery earth itself (but make sure that it has the same earth potential as the battery). Think of the chassis and body metal of the vehicle as one very large gauge "wire" connecting the earth of the battery to every earthed electrical accessory.

When earthing a component, scrape off the paint around the area you have chosen as your earth point and always use a star washer to make a good electrical connection. Star washers are better than flat washers for earthing because flat washers trap contaminants between themselves and the earthing surface, which increases contact resistance. Star washers also tend to "bite" into the earthing surface, which means the contact area between the washer and the body metal has more surface area, which means lower resistance.

Speaker wires and impedance

So-called "premium" speaker wires offer you improved "depth" and "clarity," "better dynamic range" and "tighter, deeper bass." Listening to the advertising hype about speaker wires, you'd think that "time-correct windings," "magnetic flux tube construction," "linear polyethylene dielectric," etc. are behind all this goodness. What you won't hear from the advertisements is that these benefits actually accrue from using the correct wire gauge. In addition to proper shielding, proper wire-gauge size is critical for speaker wires to assure proper speaker performance.

Amplifier	Speaker wire length	Wire gauge (SWG)
All wattages	Up to 360 cm	#18
All wattages	Up to 600 cm	#16
All wattages	Up to 900 cm	#14

As you can see, the wire gauge depends on the length of the cable: the longer the wire, the higher the resistance (and impedance) so you must compensate for the added length by installing wire of a larger gauge. Consider these gauge recommendations a starting point – when in doubt, go larger (smaller gauge number).

Interconnects

Most head units have a set of "RCA" jacks on the back that output a low-level signal. These jacks allow you to feed the signal from the head unit to an external amplifier. A high-level signal (such as the wires that run from the head unit) would overload an amp and this would likely lead to serious damage. If you're planning to run a separate amplifier, make sure that the head unit is equipped with a set of RCA outputs. Some head units have several pairs of RCA jacks, which allows you to hook up the head unit to more than one amp.

Interconnects (also known as "patch cables," "patch cords," "RCAs" and "signal cables") are not just used for carrying the low-level pre-amplified signal from the head unit to the amplifier(s). They're also used for connecting all kinds of decks (cassette, CD, DVD, video, etc.) to the head unit. On some lower-priced systems, they're also occasionally used as speaker cables. The connection itself on each end of the interconnect is known as an "RCA" (the Radio Corporation of America, which invented it). An RCA connection consists of a fat "pin" in the middle of the cable carrying the signal, surrounded by a metal barrel (which itself is usually covered in the same color plastic as the insulation on the wires). RCAs are popular with manufacturers, installers and customers because they're ridiculously easy to connect: simply plug the pin into its female counterpart on the back of the head unit, amp, deck, etc. Interconnects are available in many colors, designs, styles and configurations.

One property that is not shared by all interconnects is the degree of insulation that they provide from noise. The automotive environment is noisy, particularly if you're stringing long cables (say, from the head unit back to the boot area), or if you're wiring a low-level (less than 2-volt) pre-amp signal source or if you're using high-power amplifiers with 100 or more watts per channel. The trouble is, cable manufacturers don't exactly specify noise immunity. If you see some marketing buzzwords like "double-shielded" or "100 percent foil shield," then those interconnects probably do have better-than-average shielding from noise. But keep in mind that a noisy system is caused by numerous factors besides the type of interconnects that you use.

Another thing you *should* look for when buying interconnects to use between the head unit and the amplifier(s) is an "amplifier turn-on wire" attached down the side of the cable. This little wire, which can be used to connect the amp ON-OFF signal jack on the back of the head unit to the amp, is very handy when you're installing an amp. If you don't want to use the turn-on, you simply strip it off the side of the cable. On the other hand, if you purchase a set of interconnects *without* a turn-on already installed, and then find that you need or want one, you'll have to cut a length of 19-gauge primary wire for the amp's "remote on."

Still another thing to look for on interconnects are the directional arrows printed on the insulation jacket to indicate the direction that the signal travels (from the head unit to the amp, from a deck to the head unit, etc.). Not all interconnects are directional, but if they are you MUST install them with that in mind or they won't work correctly.

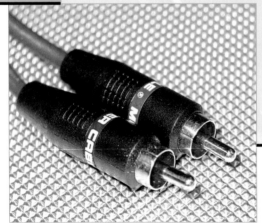

Recommended wiring installation sequence

Here's a good sequence to use when wiring up a new system:

1) Always disconnect the negative battery terminal. You don't want to damage an expensive audio component, the onboard engine management computer or some other control module by unplugging something that's still "hot."

2) Route the main power cables and decide where to put any fuses for those circuits.

3) Route the live, earth and speaker cables for each component. Be sure to leave some extra cable or wire at each end for adjustments and to give you a little slack. If you cut the cables too short, for example, you'll make it difficult to remove the head unit from the dash.

4) Route the interconnects (low-power signal cables). *Keep them as far away as possible from all power cables and factory wiring harnesses carrying more than minuscule levels of current.* Again, leave a little extra cable so that you'll be able to pull out the head unit later if necessary. It's better to leave the extra at the amps or other peripheral components instead of at the head unit. Coiling up extra signal cable at the head unit could cause noise problems. On the other hand, it is perfectly acceptable to bundle low-power signal cables together with electrical tape or cable ties in order to "clean up" your new wiring harness; there's no danger of signal cables in close proximity to one another causing a noise problem in adjacent signal cables.

5) Starting with the component that's the furthest away from the head unit and then working your way back to the head unit, make the final connections.

Fuses and circuit breakers: cheap insurance

Fuses

A fuse is a device that protects a circuit from excessive current levels. It consists of a wire or a strip of metal inside a glass or plastic housing. Fuses are installed inline with power wires that might melt down if subjected to excessive current. The strip of metal inside a fuse is designed to overheat, melt and break - *before* the wire does so - if the flow of current through the circuit exceeds the current-carrying capability of the wiring. Think of the fuses as cheap insurance.

Types of fuses

AGU fuses

The AGU fuse design has been around for awhile now. Think of the AGU as the "classic" fuse. It's a strip of metal wire inside a small glass tube with metal ends (the metal ends are connected by the wire inside the tube). The wire strip inside an AGU fuse is always a little smaller gauge than the wire it protects. When used in a fuse box or fuse panel, AGU fuses are easy to install and remove. They're also a good choice for an inline fuse because of their cylindrical shape and compact size, and inline fuse holders for AGU fuses are also compact and cheap.

ATO or blade fuses

The blade style fuse has been gaining ground for almost two decades as the fuse of choice for original factory-installed circuits and even for professional aftermarket installers. It consists of two spade terminals connected by a metal strip, which is housed inside a transparent plastic housing. Unlike the AGU fuse, which has its terminals at opposite ends, the blade type fuse has both terminals on the same side. Because you can cram a lot more blade fuses onto a fuse panel, there's not much clearance between the fuses, so it's difficult to remove this type of fuse without the special removal tool that looks like a pair of small plastic tweezers. The tool is usually stowed somewhere in the fuse panel. Blade fuses can also be used as inline fuses, with the proper holder.

Maxi fuses

Sometimes the biggest blade fuse isn't big enough. Think of maxi fuses as the big brothers to blade fuses. Maxi fuses are "slow burn" fuses, while the blade type are "fast burn" fuses.

Mini fuses

Sometimes the smallest blade fuse isn't small enough. Think of mini fuses as the little brothers of blade fuses.

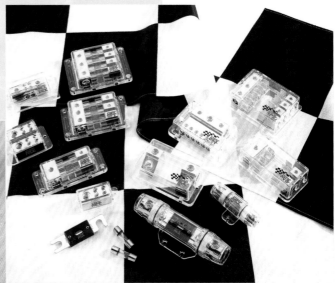

ANL and MEGA fuses

These wafer-style fuses are for applications over 80 amps.

Fuse blocks and fuse holders

Always choose a fuse block or fuse holder that accepts the wire gauge you plan to use. "Distribution" fuse blocks (one input, multiple outputs) usually accept a single 4-gauge input and have two, three or four 8-gauge outputs. High-amperage fuse holders are usually designed for 4-gauge or 8-gauge inputs and outputs. If you're buying a fuse holder for the main power line from the battery, that fuse must be no more than 25 cm from the battery, so make sure that you obtain a *waterproof* fuse holder for that application. And every time you install a fuse block or a fuse holder, make sure that you put it where it will be easy to get to in the event that you have to check it.

Circuit breakers

A circuit breaker is a device placed in series with a power line which will open the power connection when an excess amount of current is sensed, thus protecting a circuit or system. Unlike a fuse, which melts its wire when the current becomes excessive, a circuit breaker can be reset. Some reset themselves, while others must be reset manually.

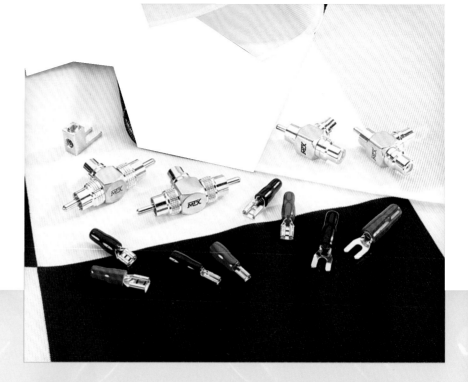

Connectors

Cars use many different types of electrical connectors for different purposes. With the increasing complexity of modern car electrical systems and the advent of computer control systems many new types of special connectors have emerged. Most mobile electronics projects involve lots of connectors. Let's take a look at the types of connections commonly used when installing automotive sound systems and mobile electronics: soldering, crimp connectors and Scotchlok connectors.

Soldering

Soldering is generally regarded as the best electrical connection. It provides low impedance, corrosion resistance and strength. But soldered connections are time-consuming, particularly if you're the impatient type, and tricky, particularly if you're untutored. Even after you have mastered the art of soldering, sometimes you just have to employ quicker and easier ways to connect wires together.

Some general guidelines for soldering

1) Always slip a section of heat-shrink tubing onto one of the wires you're going to connect before you solder the connection.

2) Use rosin-core solder in a 60-to-40 ratio (60 percent tin, 40 percent lead or the lead-free equivalent).

3) Make sure that the connection that you're going to solder is free of dirt and corrosion.

4) Be sure to "tin" the soldering iron tip occasionally by coating it with solder. Then wipe off the excess with a clean rag until the tip is smooth and silvery.

5) Heat the connection, not the solder.

6) Use the side of the soldering iron tip near the point - not the point itself - to heat the connection. This angle allows more heat transfer from the tip to the connection.

7) A correctly soldered joint is smooth and silvery, not rough and grey. Rough grey joints are called "cold" joints and are caused by movement between the two items being soldered before the solder solidifies. If a joint is cold, resolder it. (If you don't, it will create high resistance at the joint and might also eventually break.)

8) Always insulate and weatherproof the connection with heat-shrink tubing when you're done.

Crimp connectors

To make electrical connections, many professional electrical technicians use a wide variety of crimp connectors available. Crimp connectors are not as weatherproof as soldered connections, but, when you use a special crimping tool (available at most auto parts stores), making these connections is quick and easy.

Having the right type and size crimp connector handy for the wire or wires you want to connect is key when you're installing an audio system or mobile electronic components. If you use the wrong type of crimp connector, it might unplug itself over time. If you use a crimp connector that's too big for the gauge wire you're connecting, the connector might work its way off the end of the wire. Even if it stays put, the connection between the connector and the wire might be poor, resulting in unnecessarily high resistance in the circuit.

Crimp connectors are quick and easy to install - simply strip off about 0.7 cm of insulation using the proper-gauge hole on your stripping tool . . .

. . . insert the stripped wire and crimp the connector firmly onto it using the correct crimping jaws of the tool

What if the wire on which you want to install a crimp connector is too small for the connector, or one of the wires you want to connect to another wire is too small for the butt connector that fits the larger wire gauge? Beef up the thinner wire by stripping off twice as much insulation as you normally would, then fold the wire back over itself and twist it together.

If the wire on which you want to install a crimp connector is too large for the biggest crimp connector you've got handy? Then it's time to head to the nearest auto parts store for more crimp connectors! In other words, do NOT try to "cut down" the gauge of a stripped-off wire end in order to jam it into a too-small crimp connector. You will be creating a high-resistance hot spot in the circuit that will surely overheat and might even start a fire.

The following descriptions briefly summarize some of the most popular styles of crimp connectors used by installers. There are others, but the following types of crimp connectors will enable you to make nearly any type of connection you will encounter when installing an audio system or other mobile electronic components.

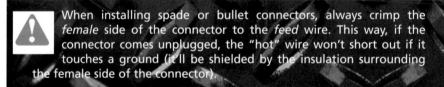

When installing spade or bullet connectors, always crimp the *female* side of the connector to the *feed* wire. This way, if the connector comes unplugged, the "hot" wire won't short out if it touches a ground (it'll be shielded by the insulation surrounding the female side of the connector).

Butt connectors

Butt connectors are used to permanently connect two wire ends together. Simply strip off about 0.7 cm of insulation from each wire, insert

the stripped ends of both wires into the opposite ends of the connector and then "crimp" the butt connector with a crimping tool. To verify the soundness of the connection, try to pull the two wires out of the connector.

Ring terminals

Ring terminals are used at the end of a wire or cable to make a secure connection to earth, terminal blocks or the battery. Installed ring terminals are mashed flat by the bolt or screw used to secure them, so they make good contact (like a washer) and almost never come loose. Ring terminals are installed just like butt connectors: simply strip off about 0.7 cm of insulation, insert the stripped end of the wire into the ring terminal, crimp the terminal firmly and then give it a good jerk to see if it's going to hold. When attaching a ring terminal to the vehicle chassis or body as earth, make sure that there's no paint or anything else between the ring terminal and the metal surface being used as a earth.

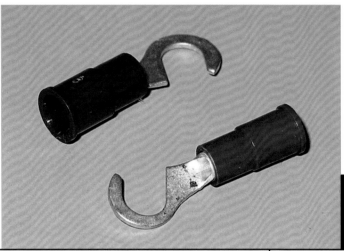

Hook terminals

Hook terminals are similar to ring terminals, but they have an open side (they're shaped like a question mark). Their advantage is that they can be connected to a terminal block more quickly than a conventional ring terminal because, while you have to loosen the screw on the terminal block, you don't have to remove it, to connect a hook terminal.

Spade connectors

A male spade connector, which looks like one of the terminals on an electrical plug, is also known as a flat-blade, quick-disconnect or push-on connector. Spade connectors are commonly used to connect accessory component wiring to the fuse panel because they're easy to plug in, and to disconnect, in tight spaces. When used with a female connector half, a spade connector also allows you to connect two wires together that must occasionally be disconnected. On the downside, they're prone to pull apart if the wiring is too tight or if there's a lot of vibration.

Spade tongue connectors

Spade tongue connectors look like a male spade terminal with its center notched out; i.e. they're U-shaped. Like hook terminals, spade tongue connectors are used to make connections to earth points or terminal blocks because they're quicker to hook up than ring terminals. But spade tongue connectors have the same disadvantage as hook terminals: they can come loose more easily than ring terminals.

Bullet connectors

Bullet connectors look like butt connectors except that they consist of a male and female side; i.e. they're always used in pairs. Bullet connectors are used to connect wires together that must be occasionally disconnected. Like spade connectors, they shouldn't be used to make permanent connections, because they can work themselves loose if the wires are too tight or if there's a lot of vibration present.

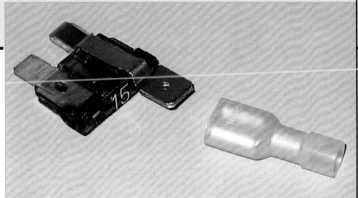

Here's a female spade connector next to a fuse fitted with a fuse tap. If you're using a fuse tap to supply power to an added component, make sure you install it on the "fused" side of the fuse. To find the proper side, remove the fuse and probe the contacts in the fuse block with a test light; the contact with NO voltage present is the proper side on which to install the fuse tap

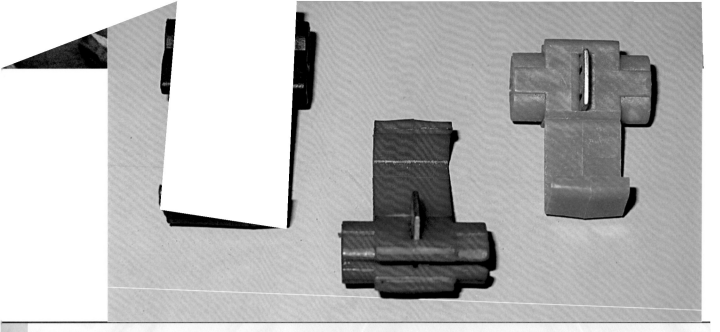

Quick-splice
connectors

The main advantage of quick-splice connectors is that you don't
have to strip off any insulation or cut any wires to make a
connection. Simply open the clamshell-style connector, place the
wire you're going to tap into and the new wire you're installing
into their respective channels, squeeze the guillotine-like blade
down into its slot (which slices through the insulation of both wires
and contacts the metal conductors of both wires), fold the clamp
over until it snaps and you're done.

01 To use a quick-splice connector, pass the "tap" wire through the outer channel of the connector . . .

02 . . . push the "run" wire (the wire that is to power the component you're installing) into the inner channel until it stops (make sure it goes past the blade, all the way to the end) . . .

03 . . . squeeze the blade into the slot . . .

04 . . . and snap the clamp into place

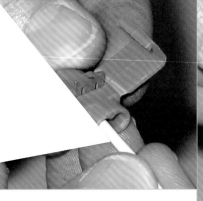 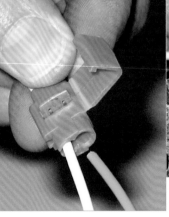  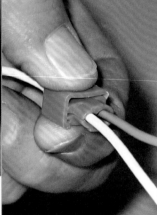

Sound-deadening
materials

Bad vibrations

Installing good speakers is the most common upgrade to a sound system because the speakers are generally regarded as the weakest link in any system. But the sound quality of automotive speakers depends to a large extent on the quality of the installation, which in turn depends on the craftsmanship, skills and techniques of the installer. That's because a motor vehicle isn't really the best place to mount a speaker.

A speaker transforms electrical energy into mechanical energy, which is in turn transformed into acoustical energy, which is radiated outward (into the car and the listeners' ears). Let's call this the front wave. But the speaker also radiates acoustical energy in the other direction, too. Let's call this the back wave. The speaker frame also transmits energy into its mounting surface, which acts like a big, not-too-flexible "speaker cone." If the vibrations of the back wave and the random vibrations of the mounting surface aren't contained and controlled, you get distortion.

The only way to get the optimum performance from good quality speakers is to quiet-down the surfaces around and behind the speakers. Installing sound-deadening material in a few strategic places is one of the most cost-effective upgrades you can make to your audio system. Aside from reducing or eliminating buzzes and rattles in the doors and other areas, it will insulate the highly reflective sheet metal surfaces which act like a mirror to the back wave coming off the speakers, which then bounce back and interfere with the front wave. Although you'll never be able to transform your vehicle into a recording studio, the more interior surfaces you treat with sound-deadening material, the better results you'll get from your speakers.

Kill the echo!

01 One sound-deadening material is Dynamat Xtreme, installed here to the inner door panel. The door now essentially becomes a much more efficient "speaker box"

02 Other flat surfaces can be treated to some sound deadening material to insulate the interior from outside noise and to prevent sound waves from bouncing around when they shouldn't. It's very easy to install - the hardest part is taking off the trim panels and cleaning the sheet metal!

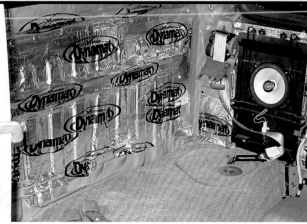

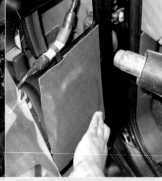

03 Another sound-deadening material is Black Hole Pad, a thin black flexible viscoelastic deadening material (filled vinyl copolymer) for installing high-end speakers in the doors. First, remove the door trim panel and the plastic moisture barrier, as well as the speakers you're going to replace (refer to your Haynes manual for help). Then make sure that the surface on which you're going to apply the deadening material is free of dirt, dust and moisture. Wipe off this area with a suitable degreaser

04 To make the material more flexible for mounting, place the material outside to allow the sun to soften it up for a few minutes before applying. Then cut a slightly oversized piece for the speaker opening . . .

05 . . . place the oversized piece directly on the speaker opening and cut it again, to a more precise fit

06 Peel off the adhesive backing and apply the deadening material to the door. Using a heat gun, heat the material slightly while applying pressure to the sheet so that the material conforms to the door's surface

Black Hole 5 is a thick multi-layered material that dampens, isolates and absorbs sound energy. Applying a multi-layered deadening material to the inside of a door panel or cabinet can improve the overall sound quality coming from the speaker. Start by cutting out two "doughnuts"

07 Using a razor blade, cut the material from the speaker opening

08

09 Remove the adhesive backing from a doughnut . . .

10 . . . then apply it to the backside of the door panel. The door is now ready for speaker installation

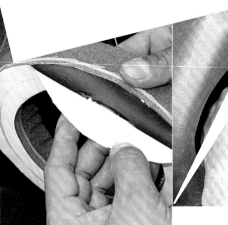

Power aerial

**Is your power aerial broken?
Try swapping it out with an aftermarket
power aerial replacement**

Universal-fit motorised aerials are available to replace
an existing, broken motorised aerial, or to install in
place of a fixed mast aerial. Check out the following
replacement procedure - it's general in nature, but it'll give you a
good idea of what to expect.

Installing a power aerial

First, unscrew the aerial
retaining nut. The special
spanner wrench you see here,
which is available from most
auto parts stores, makes this job
easier. If you can't get a hold of
one, a pair of needle-nose pliers,
with the tips engaged
with the slots in the nut,
will work

The vehicle on which we're replacing the aerial uses a rear-
mount location on the left rear quarter panel, so we started
by removing the trim panel from the luggage
compartment. (If you need help with this task, refer to
the Haynes manual for your car)

01

02

03 Disconnect the
electrical connector
from the aerial

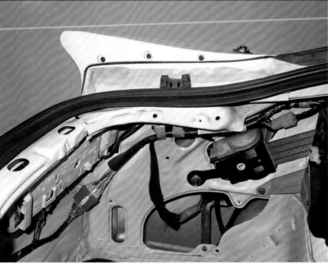

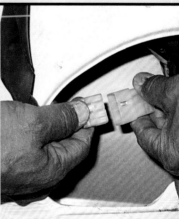

04 Remove the mounting bolt for the old aerial mounting bracket

05 Lower the aerial and disconnect the drain tube from the bottom of the motor housing. Also disconnect the aerial lead. Now remove the old aerial

06 Remove the retainer from the old aerial . . .

07 . . . and install it on the new aerial

08 Carefully guide the new aerial into place

09 Install a new rubber gasket . . .

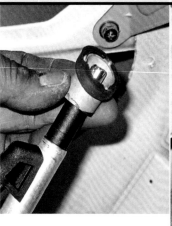

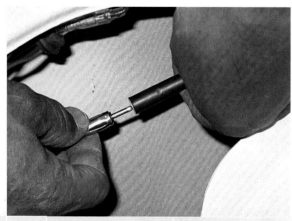

10 . . . followed by the base (the installation kit should contain a variety of bases - choose the one with the proper angle to best fit the contours of your vehicle)

11 Next, install the washer and the new aerial nut, tightening it securely

12 Connect the aerial lead to the aerial connector on the new power aerial. Also connect the drain tube

13 Attach the new mounting bracket to the aerial, then bend it into shape so it's in close proximity to the mounting hole in the body panel

14 Slide on a "quick fastener" (sheet metal clip) . . .

15 . . . insert a metal screw and tighten it securely

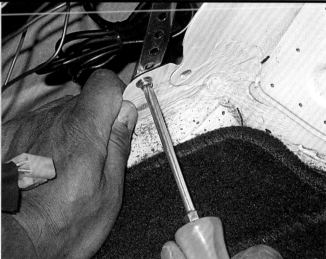

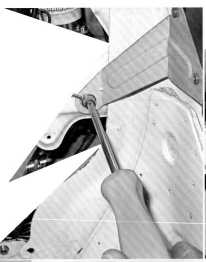

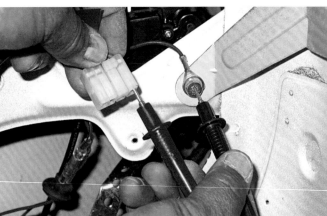

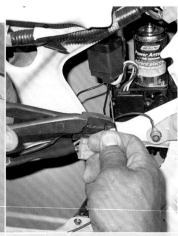

16 Attach the earth wire to a good earth. (Sheet metal brackets like this one are usually good earth points because they're bolted to the body, so the fasteners are usually making good contact with the body metal - if necessary, sand off some paint to get a good connection)

17 Grab your voltmeter. You're going to identify some terminals in the remaining half of the aerial harness electrical connector (the vehicle side of the old connector) First, find the terminal that has a constant 12-volts. This is the live wire for the aerial motor. Then find the terminal that is switched on and off when the radio is turned on and off. This is the signal wire from the radio that tells the motor to raise the aerial when the radio is turned on, and to lower it when the radio is turned off. Have a friend turn the radio on and off while you verify that the voltage goes from zero to 12V when the radio is turned on, and goes back to zero when the radio is turned off

18 Once you've identified the live and signal terminals in the old connector, set it aside for a moment and look at the electrical leads on the new aerial assembly. There should be three wires: one for live, one for the signal and the earth wire (which you've already attached to a earth). Our aerial has a red live wire and a blue signal wire (colors will vary with the manufacturer). Cut off the excess wire on each lead; leave just enough so that neither wire is too tight

19 Strip off about 0.7 to 1.0 cm of insulation from the end of each wire and crimp on a couple of male spade terminals that will fit the female receptacles of the old connector

20 Plug the new spade terminals for the live and signal wires into their corresponding terminals in the old connector. Then hop in the car, turn on the radio and verify that the aerial mast goes up when you do so. Then turn off the radio and make sure that the mast goes down

21 Secure the connector to the body panel with a cable tie and generally tidy up the harness by taping or cable-tying it to the body

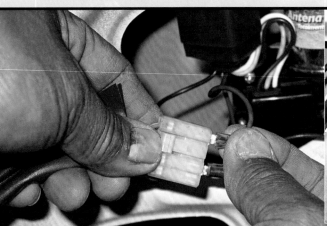

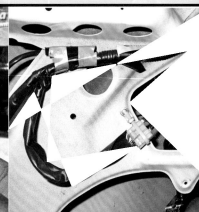

Look Mum, no hands!

As of December 2003 (okay, March 2004 really) it became illegal to hold your mobile while driving. Well, brilliant - something new to get done for. Like we were really getting short of that kind of thing. But you have to say, yipping and driving always was a pretty dodgy pastime, with driving coming off worse - if only all the UK's traffic legislation made this much sense.

Of course, the people who really benefit are the ones making hands-free car phone kits - you're looking at upwards of £50 (for a conventional kit) to get anything worth fitting. Which one do I go for? Will I have to make holes in my dash? Good questions. But we're jumping ahead - let's deal first with what the new law means in the real world.

Points of law

First, fitting a hands-free kit is merely a way of getting round part of the new legislation. They're not 'fully-legal', they're just 'not prohibited'. Even using a hands-free set-up is a distraction while you're piloting your machine, and if you start weaving about, carve up a cyclist, or run a red light, you're still likely to face a 'driving without due care' charge, or worse. The best solution for making a call is to stop where it's safe - have voicemail enabled if you get called while you're driving.

Answering a call, even with hands-free, might not be safe in all circumstances. Let it ring. As for what you're allowed to do with the phone itself - it's just pressing the buttons (and no, this doesn't mean it's ok 2 txt). Holding the phone in any way is not permitted. Even if you're stuck in traffic, completely stationary, the engine would have to be off before you can use your mobile normally - only then could you really say you weren't 'driving'.

At the moment, getting caught using a phone on the move only carries a fixed fine. But it looks like this hasn't worked, because it's soon going to be a bigger fine, and points on the licence. Use your moby sensibly (better still, don't use it, in the car at least), or it could mean re-sitting your driving test. Paying attention now, aren'tcha?

Achtung!
Don't just pull over and screech to a stop when the phone rings. If you do this somewhere stupid, you're just as likely to get fined as you would for using the phone on the move.

tricks 'n' tips
If you've got a passenger in the car, it's perfectly legal for them to use a mobile, so if yours rings, let them answer it, and relay the message to you - can't be done for that.

What's available?

Conventional kits

The new law has brought a whole range of new product to the market, so there's no need to settle for the old-style in-car kits, which leave holes all over your dash. Most of the latest kits have adhesive pads, and just plug into your fag lighter. The most essential item, to comply with the rules, is a phone holder or 'cradle' (holding phone bad - cradle good).

As no-one keeps the same phone for very long, it's worth looking for a kit which you can convert from one make of phone to another - by buying a different adapter lead, for instance.

Look for kits offering 'full duplex' operation - this means you can talk and listen at the same time. Just like real life. What it really means is conversations are easier and more natural - to understand fully why you need this feature, try one without it. Non-duplex kits cut out the speaker when they pick up any sound - this could be you talking (as intended), or it could just be noise inside the car. Very irritating, especially in an area where you've already got poor reception to deal with.

Some kits feature 'infra-red technology', which means you can answer/end calls by waving your hand in front of the phone. Proper hands-free operation, and great for impressing your passengers. Maybe not so good if you make lots of hand gestures while driving?

Car stereo kits

One of the newest ideas, and catching on fast. Uses a radio transmitter clipped over the phone speaker to transmit calls over a radio channel on your car stereo. When the phone rings, flick on the radio to the preset channel, speak into the phone's mike as normal, and hear your caller through your car speakers (since it's your stereo, you have easy control over call volume). They're cheap, and they appear to work, though there are potential problems with interference. Remember, this is a developing technology - it pays to buy the latest model you can find.

Bluetooth headsets

Bluetooth offers wireless operation, so get yourself a headset with mike, and you can chat away without having the phone up to your ear. Most modern handsets are Bluetooth-capable, and really new ones also have voice-activated dialling, which offers true hands-free operation in the car. Downsides? Some doubts over sound quality, and do you really want to wear a headset all the time you're driving?

Kit fitting

Fitting details are obviously going to vary, depending on what you've bought – the main trick is to get one which doesn't require you to go drilling holes in your dash. Luckily, this is now so unpopular that most modern kits don't even offer hole-drilling as an option.

Pama Plug n Go

This is one neat unit – no dangling wires, a well-designed mounting bracket with a huge sucker for sticking to the windscreen, and a built-in speaker which faces the glass, so sound is 'reflected' back. The unit is self-contained, with a built-in battery (car charger supplied), so it can be used anywhere, not just in-car. Looks sweet, works a treat.

Jabra Bluetooth headset

Only any good to you if your phone's got Bluetooth, but like the Pama unit we fitted earlier, there's no mess. The headset needs charging before use, but after that, you just 'pair' your phone and headset together, and start jabbering. If your phone's trendy enough to have voice-activated dialling, this is about as hands-free as you'll get. You don't even need a cradle for your mobile with this one!

Mr Handsfree

01 All these kits (apart from the Bluetooth headset) need power, usually conveniently taken from the fag lighter socket. Umm, yeah... right... Not easy getting the adapter in the socket, with the ashtray in place, is it?

02 If you're not going to drill holes, you'll be sticking stuff on. If you want things to stay stuck (and you usually only get one shot at this) a little cleaning is in order first.

03 Mostly, it's Velcro pads you get for sticking the various kit bits in place (so they can be easily ripped off and stashed when you leave the car). Leave the two 'halves' of Velcro stuck together while fitting. With the mounting area clean, it's peel . . .

04 . . . and press firmly. This is the main unit, which contains the speaker. We thought the centre console was too good a spot to ignore. You only have to ensure the two curly-cords will reach the lighter socket and the phone.

05 Not all fitting is quite this simple, though. With a little clever thinking, you can do a much neater fitting job than one which leaves all the wires hanging out. Take this little mike which comes with the Mr Handsfree kit – by prising out one of the blank switches, we hid the wire inside the dash and stuck the mike to the switch, right where it's needed. Result.

06 For mounting the phone itself, we have a magnetic bracket, again stuck with sticky pads. It's only an old Nokia, but we'd still better make sure it doesn't hit the deck, by making sure it's firmly attached.

07 And there it is – the phone's nice and handy, the mike's discreetly mounted, and the speaker unit's tucked in the console. And this is the first one of these we've fitted!

Fitting an auxiliary fusebox

You'll need plenty of fused live feeds from the battery during the modifying process, for stereo gear, neons, starter buttons - and alarms, and it's always a pain working out where to tap into one. If you make up your own little fusebox, mounted somewhere easy to get at, you'll never have this problem again - and it's easy enough to do.

The first job is to run a main supply cable from the battery positive terminal, to inside the car - but don't connect the wire up to the battery terminal just yet. Make sure that the main cable is man enough for all the loads you're likely to put on it - starting with eight-gauge wire (available from all good ICE suppliers) will mean you're never short of current.

Make a note of which fuse is for which circuit, and carry the paper around in the glovebox (along with some spare fuses). If a fuse ever blows, you won't end up with your head stuck under the dash, trying to remember where you tapped in, and where the fuse is. You'll just pull the cover off, and replace the fuse. Who would've thought electrical safety could be so cool?

01 First job is to find a suitable place to locate the fusebox. We've chosen the floor area under the passenger seat to locate ours - easily accessible in the event a blown fuse, and out of the way. Place the boxes on a flat area of floor, and in such a way that the forward/backward movement of the seat is not affected. Next, create paper templates of the two boxes, and transfer them to card.

02 Place the card template in position and cut out the shape. Then repeat process for other box - ensure at least a four-inch gap between the two boxes, to allow some wire-connection room.

07 Push the grommet back into place. Might be a good idea to treat it to some silicone sealant, to keep the elements out - after all, if you get water trickling down that new wire, where's it going to end up? Oops.

08 Next job is to connect the cable to the positive terminal of the battery using a ring terminal. Make sure you do a decent job here - there could be a load of accessories depending on it. Take care once that lead goes onto the battery, too - the business end inside the car will be live.

09 Inside the car again, and pick up the cable we threaded through the bulkhead. To tidily route the wire to the junction box, the sill trim and carpet will have to be pulled up and out of the way. Fortunately, this is easy - prise the sill trim up, and remove two seat belt rail retaining bolts.

10 With the carpet lifted up, thread the cable down the car. For a neat job, hold the wire in place with some tape.

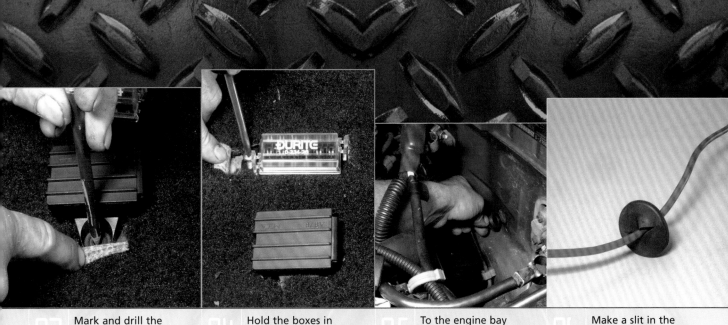

03 Mark and drill the mounting holes of the two boxes. Check underneath the car before commencing drilling – avoid fuel lines and such like!

04 Hold the boxes in place using self-tapping screws. If you're really lucky, you might find those same screws could be used as earth points, giving you ready-made lives and earths in the same place - how clever is that?

05 To the engine bay now, to find a path for the wire to travel from the battery through the bulkhead, down the car into the fusebox. As luck would have it – a perfectly-situated grommet underneath the battery!

06 Make a slit in the grommet and thread your wire through the slit (the cable must be at least eight-gauge if lots of loads are going on it). It's a good idea at this point to make sure you have a long enough cable to reach down to the fusebox under the seat as well as extending up to the battery - don't cut the wire from the reel until you're sure.

11 We could've joined the single live feed to the six wires of the fusebox, using a large bullet connector, or a terminal block. Both of these options are a little dodgy, so we bought a junction box from the same place as our fusebox. Pop open the junction box to see the two nut-and-bolt connection terminals - it's a much simpler and safer solution. Crimp a ring terminal to the end of the cable, and fix to the left terminal of junction box.

12 Next cut six lengths of wire (long enough to reach fusebox), and solder all six wires to a ring terminal. To protect the wires we added some heat shrink as well - no such thing as too much electrical safety. Then fix the ring connector to the right-hand terminal of the junction box.

13 Crimp connectors onto the ends of each of the six wires, and slot them into place on the fusebox. Then as and when you need a live feed, you can take a feed wire from whatever you're fitting and connect it to one of the fusebox terminals – simple-as.

14 Oh, and don't forget to add the correct fuse – otherwise your efforts were in vain! You might need some guesswork as to the right fuse rating for some accessories, but don't just go for the biggest fuse you can every time. Remember to pop the fusebox cover back on, too.

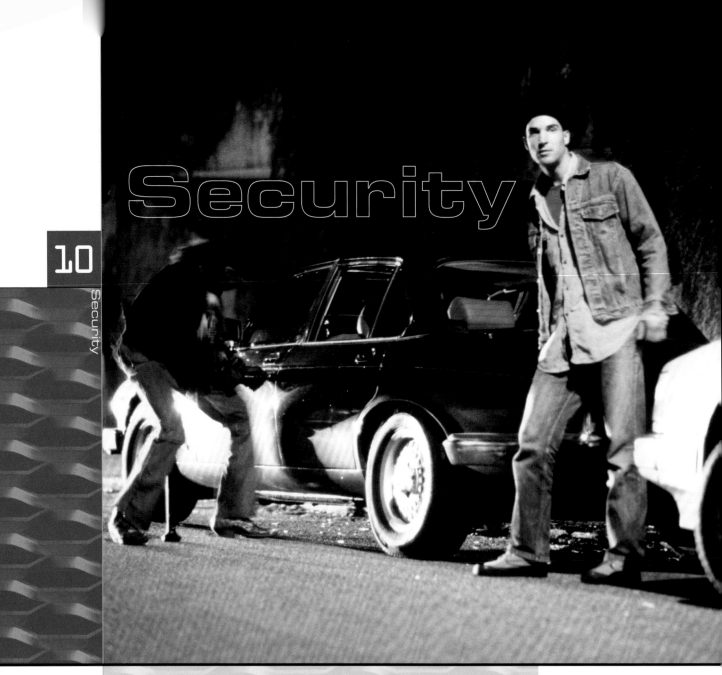

Security

Avoiding trouble

Those shiny wheels and flashy paint are like a billboard to car thieves and bandits looking for expensive sound system components to sell on the black market. So you've got to be careful when and where you choose to show off your car's mobile entertainment, and to whom. Be especially discreet the nearer you get to home - turn your system down before you get near home, for instance, or you might draw unwelcome attention to where that car with the loud stereo's parked at night!

If you're going out, think about where you're parking - somewhere well-lit and reasonably well-populated is the best bet.

If you're lucky enough to have a garage, use it. Always use all the security you have, whenever you leave the car, even if it's a tedious chore to put on that steering wheel lock. Just do it.

Alarm systems

There are many different types of automotive alarm systems, ranging from simple and inexpensive systems to complex and costly ones. But most alarm systems use a combination of the following components: a control unit, a siren, "switch triggers" and/or sensors, an engine "immobiliser" and a remote control unit. Let's take a quick look at the function of, and application for, each of these components, so when a salesman starts throwing around technical terms like "switch trigger" or "radio field disturbance sensor," you'll at least have some idea what he's talking about.

But don't rely on salesmen as your only source of information. Talk to your friends too. Ask them what type of security systems they're using on their cars, where they bought it, how much it cost, how long they've had it, how well it's worked so far, etc. Before purchasing an alarm system, be sure to give yourself plenty of time to study a system you might want to buy so that you'll understand its advantages and shortcomings when compared to other similarly priced systems. Car shows are a good place to see security systems installed on demo vehicles by the manufacturers. The people who work the shows always know most everything about the products they sell.

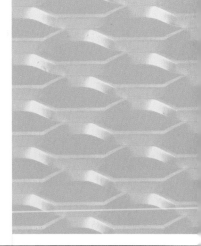

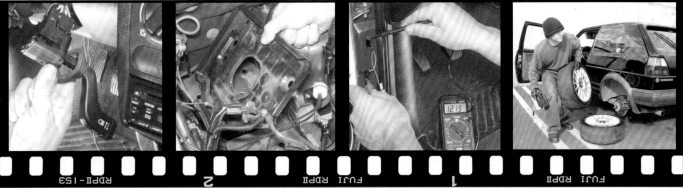

Control unit

The control unit is the "brain" of the alarm system. It controls all functions of the security system, such as arming and disarming the system, monitoring the switch triggers and/or sensors and processing this data to determine the threat level. If the real deal goes down, the control unit responds in accordance with the level of the threat indicated by the data from the switch triggers and/or sensors. Most control units are also capable of enabling and disabling the operation of the engine. Some units even indicate the status of the system, either through LED lights or through audible beepers. When you arm or disarm the security alarm system, the control unit chirps the siren, blinks the parking lights and/or beeps the alarm to verify that the system status has just been changed.

Siren

Electronic sirens are the most common audible devices used on alarm systems. A typical modern siren consists of an oscillator (also known as a tone generator), an amplifier and a speaker. Most sirens are shaped like a bell or horn because that shape makes for a louder siren and because it improves the pitch. Some sirens are made of metal, but most of them are high-temperature plastic.

Switch triggers and sensors

Different alarm systems are characterised mainly by what type of switch triggers or sensors they use. There are a lot of different types of monitoring devices used in various alarm systems, but they fall into the following categories. There are five types of switch triggers: spring-loaded pin switches, roller push-button switches, magnetic reed switches, metal pressure switches and mercury tilt switches. There are four basic types of sensors: motion sensors, shock and impact sensors, sound discriminators and sound sensors.

Switch triggers

The **spring-loaded pin switch** consists of a spring-loaded plastic plunger inside a cylindrical metal housing with a set of contacts at the end opposite the plunger. Pin switches typically monitor the doors, hood and/or trunk. Pin switches are normally open, but if a door, bonnet, or boot lid is opened while the security system is armed, they close the circuit and activate the alarm.

The **roller push-button switch** is similar to the spring-loaded pin switch except that it uses a ball or "roller" instead of a straight linear plunger to close the switch contacts. Roller switches work better than pin switches in some applications, such as sliding doors on vans or tailgates on trucks.

The **magnetic reed switch** (also known as a **magnetic proximity switch**) uses magnetic force to close the switch contacts. A pair of magnetic "reeds" (actually two thin and flexible slivers of metal), each with a contact at one end, is housed inside a glass cylinder. The reeds are insulated from each other and are attached to a stationary point at one end. Each reed is connected to a wire, which runs outside the cylinder. The reed switch assembly is protected by a plastic case. A small permanent magnet is housed inside a similar plastic case. When the magnet part of the switch is brought near the reed assembly, the reeds are moved by the force of the magnetic field to either make (normally open switch) or break (normally closed switch) an electrical connection. Magnetic reed switches are used in applications such as sliding glass windows on pick-up truck cabs.

The **metal pressure switch** (also referred to as a **seat sensor** or **floor mat senso**r) consists of two parallel strips of brass or aluminum positioned close to one another, but insulated from one another by a strip of rubber or foam with cutouts in it. When enough pressure is applied to the two strips to press them together, the rubber or foam compresses and allows continuity. The metal pressure switch is used for sensing pressure applied to a seat cushion or a floor mat. Before the advent of spatial sensors, metal pressure switches were the only devices available for protecting open vehicles such as Jeeps.

The **mercury tilt switch** (or simply **mercury switch**) consists of a set of contacts and a small amount of mercury sealed inside a glass tube. Mercury is a good conductor of electricity, so when it touches the two electrical contacts, it completes the circuit between them. The mercury switch works on the principle of gravity: When the heavy mercury moves to the end of the cylinder containing the contacts, the circuit is closed. Mercury switches are used to detect a change in the angle of a hatch or panel in relation to the horizontal plane. Typical applications include hatchbacks and hinged rear windows openings that must be moved to a steep angle with respect to the horizontal plane.

Sensors

A **motion sensor** detects (you guessed it!) motion, more specifically, the *kind* and *degree* of motion that a vehicle might undergo if it were being jacked up or being readied for towing. What kinds of motion? Subtle and near vertical up-and-down motions, i.e. the type produced by a vehicle being jacked up. Or a gradual change in the vehicle's angle in relation to the ground, i.e. the type of change that occurs when the front or back of the vehicle is lifted for towing.

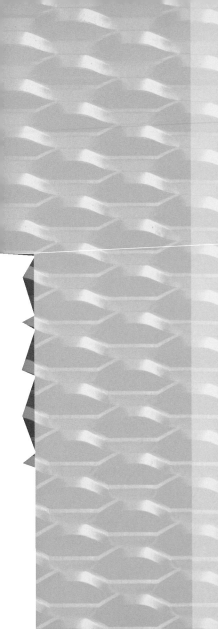

More sophisticated alarms utilise **shock and impact sensors,** which could be activated by a thief attempting to steal your tyres or trying to break into your car. Shock and impact sensors react to any shock, impact or vibration applied to a vehicle. There are so many different types of shock and impact sensors that space doesn't permit a complete description of all the various types. One common design is the **two-stage electromagnetic shock sensor**. When it detects a vibration in the vehicle, it signals the control unit, which responds in accordance to the strength of the signal. The sensor delivers a "warning trigger" signal for a light impact (maybe somebody simply bumped your car) or it can signal the control unit to go into full red alert for a harder impact (like somebody trying to prise the door lock). The installer can adjust the impact level on some of these sensors.

The third type of sensor, the **sound discriminator** (or **glass sensor**) is designed to detect the sound of breaking glass. The typical sound discriminator uses a microphone that responds to the frequency that glass produces when it breaks. The mike is connected to a filter/sampling network, which can make a finer discrimination and then select only the signature sound of glass breaking. The circuit then goes through a "comparator" which compares the level of the sound to the sensitivity threshold setting of the sensor, then decides whether to produce a trigger or not.

Sound sensors are usually **spatial sensors**, i.e. they monitor an area of "space" in the vehicle, around its perimeter, or both. There are three types of spatial sensors: ultrasonic, radio field disturbance and infrared field disturbance. **Ultrasonic sensors** were the first sensors used in vehicle security systems. An ultrasonic sensor consists of two separate sections - the sender and the receiver. The sender unit emits extremely high frequency, or ultrasonic, sound waves (10,000 Hz to 90,000 Hz) and the receiver receives them. If someone or something of sufficient mass moves into or across the space between the sender and the receiver, the change in the sound waves caused by this interruption will cause the alarm to sound.

Radio field disturbance sensors, which are by far the most common type of spatial sensor, work essentially the same way as ultrasonic sensors, except that they use even higher frequencies, in the giga (1,000,000,000) Hertz range (that's one thousand million Hertz!). Radio frequencies in this range are typically referred to as "microwaves."

Infrared field disturbance sensors are less common in vehicle security applications than other spatial sensors. They use infrared waves, which are just beyond the visible red end of the light spectrum. Infrared field disturbance sensors are particularly useful in situations where the spatial sensor must ignore any changes in air pressure, such as a convertible with the top down or any other type of vehicle open to the air.

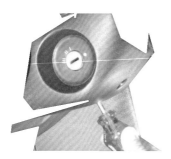

Engine immobiliser

The engine immobiliser is a device that prevents the engine from starting, or prevents it from running for more than a few seconds after it has been started. The three most common immobilisers are starter immobilisers, ignition immobilisers and fuel delivery immobilisers. A starter immobiliser interrupts or disables the starter circuit. An engine immobiliser allows a thief to operate the starter, but disables the ignition system, so the engine won't start. A fuel system immobiliser allows the engine to start but it cuts off the fuel supply, so the engine dies quickly.

Remote controls

Speaking of immobilisers, you will need a remote control unit to enable and disable the alarm system. There are three basic types of remotes: Radio Frequency (RF), infrared (IR) and inductive or magnetic. Radio frequency transmitters are the most common type of remote control unit, although they are not legal in every country. The transmitter uses radio waves of a specific frequency to turn various functions of the security system on and off. Most RF-type control units use a frequency between 300 and 470 MHz. Infrared or IR control units, unlike RF-types, must be operated within line of sight of the vehicle, because the infrared radiation emitted by these units travels only in one narrow straight line. Inductive or magnetic type control units don't actually "transmit" a signal; instead, they use the electrical property of "inductance" to enable and disable the system. The "range" of this type of remote unit is limited; you must pass the remote within a few inches of a special pick-up, which is usually installed on one of the windows of the vehicle.

Options

Many security systems are expandable. If you purchase one of these systems, you can add on extra transmitters, sensors, switch triggers, etc. to the basic system to expand its security capabilities, either at the date of purchase or later as the need arises. Some systems offer optional conveniences such as keyless entry, power window control or remote starting capability. Some systems also offer an optional FM pager that keeps tabs on your car when you're physically too far away to hear the alarm if it goes off, or it can be set to silently page you without activating the siren in the vehicle. This can be a good feature in certain environments (how often have you heard alarms blaring and nobody even pays attention; they're just considered an annoyance), but do you really want to surprise a bad guy (or more than one) breaking into your car? Think about that one before you jump into a dangerous situation.

Tinted windows and dash protectors: cheap insurance

Got tinted windows? Good! Tinted windows not only protect your interior from harmful UV rays and keep it cooler; they also make it difficult for someone to see inside your car. Most professional automotive tinters offer four shades of tint: light, medium, dark and "limousine" (or simply "limo"), which is basically an opaque black when seen from outside. If you're planning to have your car's windows tinted, go as dark as you can get away with. The darker the better. But before plunking down your hard-earned green on a tint job, be sure to consult your local authorities regarding how dark you can legally go with the front and rear windows.

But what about the windscreen? It's clear, and it's definitely illegal to tint it, so how do you prevent someone from peeking through the windscreen to case your car? That's easy. Get a simple "dash protector" that you unfold and place across the inside of the windscreen to block out the sun! They don't just protect your expensive dash from the sun; they also protect the contents of your vehicle's interior from prying eyes. These inexpensive devices are available at automotive parts retailers.

Legal eagle

The law on window tinting currently is that there must be no more than a 25% reduction in light transmission through windscreens, and a limit of 30% reduction on all other glass. How the heck do you measure light reduction? Also, many cars come with tinted glass as standard - so can you fit a tinting kit on top and still be legal? Hard to know what line to take, if you're stopped by Plod - try and choose a tinting kit which is EC-approved (ask before you buy, and if you think it could be a serious issue, get a letter from the company to support the legality of the kit, to use in your defence). Some forces now take this seriously enough to have portable test equipment they can use at the roadside - if your car fails, it's an on-the-spot fine.

Anti-theft devices

Other types of anti-theft devices are available as a less expensive alternative to alarms.

An automobile equipped with a steering wheel lock or a removable steering wheel could make your car a less likely target for a thief. Also available are locking covers for the steering column which can help prevent a thief from being able to access the ignition lock, and devices that prevent the brake or clutch pedal from being depressed. Whatever your choice may be, now every time you park, at least you can relax a little. Remember, though, there's no guarantee that installing an alarm or security device will make any difference to a determined thief or mindless vandal.

If your vehicle is equipped with an alarm system or an anti-theft device, you may be eligible for discounted insurance premiums. Certain companies offer a higher percentage discount for vehicles that have more sophisticated alarm system packages. Each insurance company will have their own guidelines and insurance discounts. Contact your insurance representative for all the specific details.

An LED draws very little current, so you'll be quite safe tapping into almost any live feed you want. If you've wired in your stereo system, take a live feed from the permanent (radio memory supply) wire at the back of your head unit, or have a delve into the back of the fusebox with your test light. An earth can easily be tapped again from your head unit, or you can make one almost anywhere on the metal body of the car, by drilling a small hole, fitting a self-tapping screw, then wrapping the bared end of wire around and tightening it.

The best and easiest place to mount an LED is into one of the many blank switches the manufacturers seem to love installing. The blank switch is easily prised out, and a hole can then be drilled to take the LED (which usually comes in a separate little holder). Feed the LED wiring down behind the dashboard to where you've tapped your live and earth, taking care not to trap it anywhere, nor to accidentally wrap it around any moving parts.

Connect your live to the LED red wire, then rig your earth to one side of the switch, and connect the LED black wire to the other switch terminal. You should now have a switchable LED. Tidy up the wiring, and mount the switch somewhere discreet, but where you can still get at it. Switch on when you leave the car, and it looks as if you've got some sort of alarm - better than nothing.

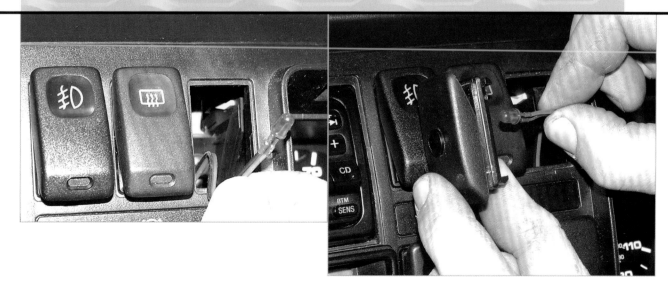

Alarm installation

In order to try and make this section as useful as possible, we won't show in detail how one particular alarm is installed, but instead pick out some of the highlights and tips that are common to most systems, in case your chosen alarm is different from ours.

01 Disconnect the cable from the negative battery terminal, and move the cable away from the battery. This will probably wipe out your stereo settings, but it's better than having sparks flying and your new alarm chirping during installation.

02 Decide where you're going to mount the alarm/siren. Choose somewhere not easily reached from underneath. Try the siren in position before deciding. It's also best to pick a location away from where you'll be adding fluids to the window washer reservoir, oil to the engine or coolant to the radiator. Loosely fit the alarm to the bracket, to help you decide how well it'll fit in your chosen spot, then take the alarm away.

03 Mark the position of the mounting holes.

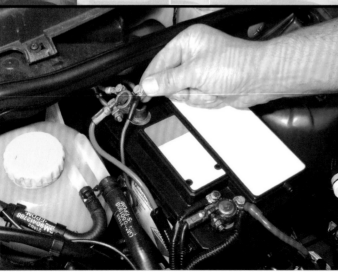

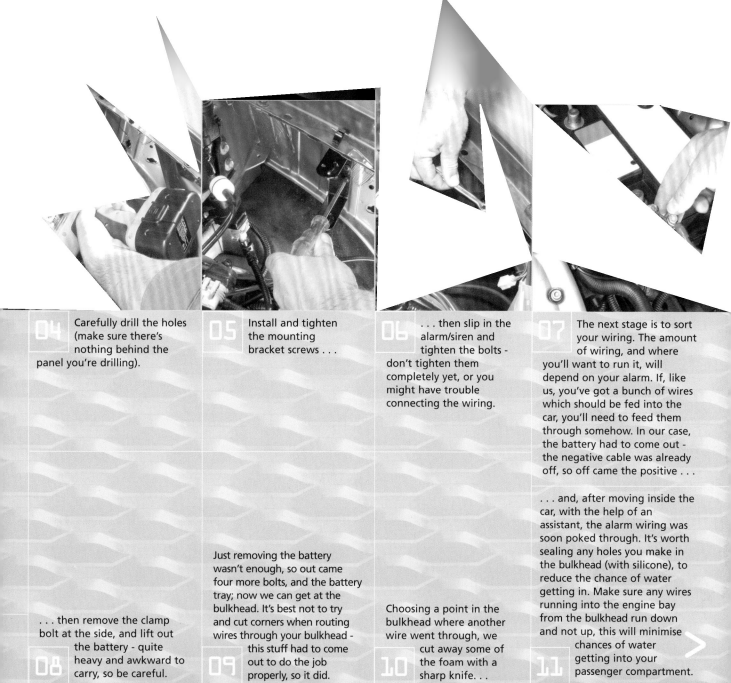

04 Carefully drill the holes (make sure there's nothing behind the panel you're drilling).

05 Install and tighten the mounting bracket screws . . .

06 . . . then slip in the alarm/siren and tighten the bolts - don't tighten them completely yet, or you might have trouble connecting the wiring.

07 The next stage is to sort your wiring. The amount of wiring, and where you'll want to run it, will depend on your alarm. If, like us, you've got a bunch of wires which should be fed into the car, you'll need to feed them through somehow. In our case, the battery had to come out - the negative cable was already off, so off came the positive . . .

. . . and, after moving inside the car, with the help of an assistant, the alarm wiring was soon poked through. It's worth sealing any holes you make in the bulkhead (with silicone), to reduce the chance of water getting in. Make sure any wires running into the engine bay from the bulkhead run down and not up, this will minimise chances of water getting into your passenger compartment.

08 . . . then remove the clamp bolt at the side, and lift out the battery - quite heavy and awkward to carry, so be careful.

09 Just removing the battery wasn't enough, so out came four more bolts, and the battery tray; now we can get at the bulkhead. It's best not to try and cut corners when routing wires through your bulkhead - this stuff had to come out to do the job properly, so it did.

10 Choosing a point in the bulkhead where another wire went through, we cut away some of the foam with a sharp knife. . .

11

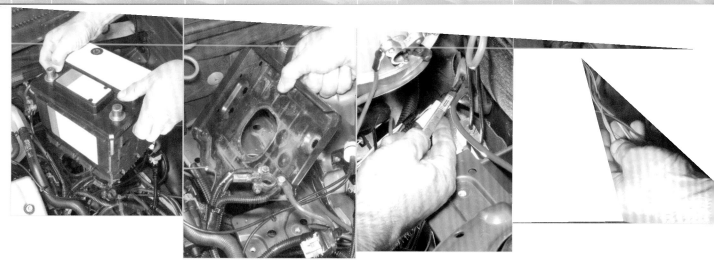

12 Routing the wires across the inside of the car to the fuse panel is easier if you tape them up – just a short piece of tape every few inches or so will keep them nicely bundled. Keeping the wires clear of the pedals might mean generous use of cable-ties.

13 Now that the wiring's more or less in the right place, it's time to start connecting it up. Power and earths can be sourced from the fuse panel - remove the screws and lower the fuse panel from the dash. It's a good idea to refer to the wiring diagrams in the Haynes manual for your vehicle, so you know which fuse to aim for in the fuse panel, and which colour wire you're after. Most of it can be decided fairly simply. When you've found a likely suspect, use a 12-volt test light (available at just about any auto parts store) or voltmeter to confirm your suspicions.

14 If you're after an ignition power circuit, probe the wire with the voltmeter or test light tip (or push it carefully into the back of the wiring connector) and attach the clip to a good earth (like one of the door pin switch screws) - check that it's a switched circuit, not a permanent, by turning the ignition on and off. To check for a earth, use the same method, but connect the clip to a 12-volt supply. It's best to tap into the fused side of any wire - to check for this, pull the fuse from the fuse panel, and make sure your chosen wire goes dead.

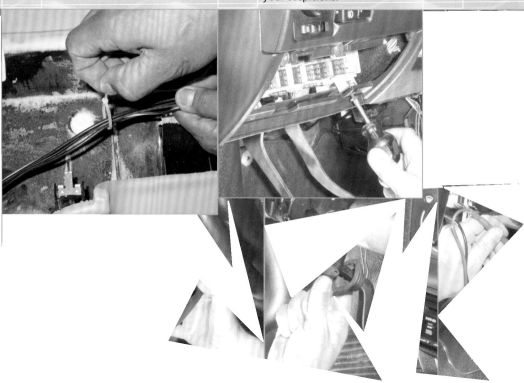

19 With a bit of persuasion, we removed the lower column cover.

20 Remove the turn signal switch for access to the wiring.

21 Use a voltmeter or test light to see which wires are live when the turn signals are switched on – check both left and right-hand turn signals.

⚠ Warning:

Whenever working on a vehicle equipped with an airbag (or airbags), be sure to disable the airbag system before working in the vicinity of any airbag system components. This is especially important when working around the instrument panel and center console. Consult the Haynes Service and Repair Manual for your vehicle for the airbag disabling procedure. If no manual exists, consult a dealer service department or other qualified repair shop to obtain the information. Also, NEVER splice or tap into any wiring for the airbag system, and never use a test light or multimeter on airbag system wiring. On most vehicles the wiring for the airbag system is yellow, or is covered by yellow conduit, or at the very least will have yellow electrical connectors.

15 Most alarms are wired into the interior light circuit, which is operated by push-switches mounted in the door pillars. To get the wiring, unscrew the driver's door switch or remove the screw holding the switch in place, and pull the switch out.

16 Disconnect the wiring plug from the switch, then use a test light to identify which of the two wires is live, and which is earth. Different alarms require you to wire into the interior light circuit on one wire or the other - check the instructions with your system.

17 Most alarms require you to link into the turn signal circuit, so the lights flash during arming and disarming. One obvious place to tap into the indicators is at the turn signal switch, which means removing the steering column covers.

18 Here we turned the wheel 90-degrees one way, then removed the screw. Turn the wheel back straight, then 90-degrees the other way, and removed the screw on the other side of the shrouds.
    Check your service manual for steering column cover removal, if necessary.

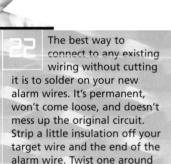

22 The best way to connect to any existing wiring without cutting it is to solder on your new alarm wires. It's permanent, won't come loose, and doesn't mess up the original circuit. Strip a little insulation off your target wire and the end of the alarm wire. Twist one around the other, if possible.

23 Now bring in the soldering iron, heat the connection, and join the wires together with solder (be careful not to burn yourself, the dash, or the surrounding wires!).

24 Remember - whatever method you use for joining the new wires (and especially if you're soldering) - insulate the new connection big-time. The last thing you want is false alarms, other electrical problems, or even a fire, caused by poorly-insulated connections.

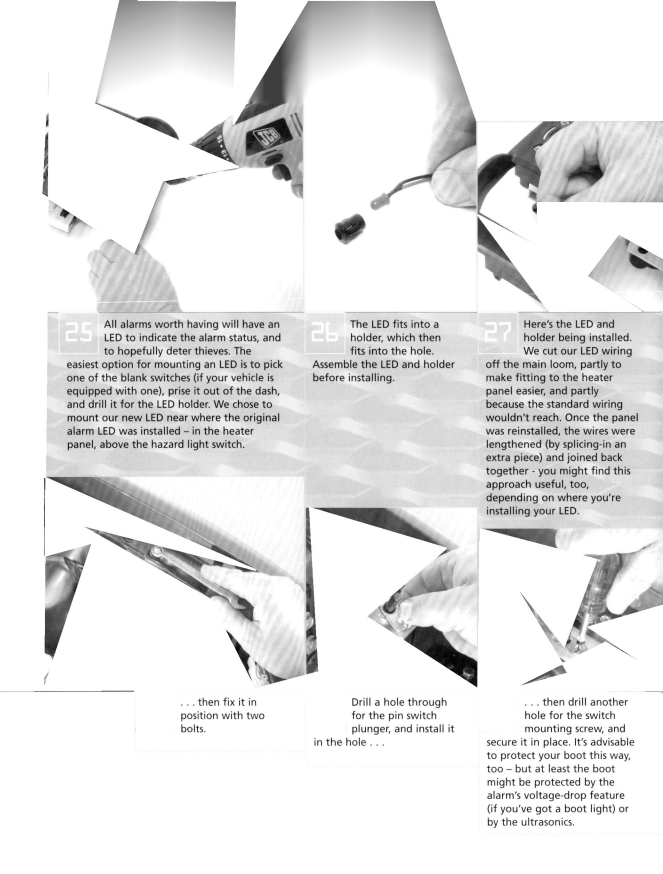

25 All alarms worth having will have an LED to indicate the alarm status, and to hopefully deter thieves. The easiest option for mounting an LED is to pick one of the blank switches (if your vehicle is equipped with one), prise it out of the dash, and drill it for the LED holder. We chose to mount our new LED near where the original alarm LED was installed – in the heater panel, above the hazard light switch.

26 The LED fits into a holder, which then fits into the hole. Assemble the LED and holder before installing.

27 Here's the LED and holder being installed. We cut our LED wiring off the main loom, partly to make fitting to the heater panel easier, and partly because the standard wiring wouldn't reach. Once the panel was reinstalled, the wires were lengthened (by splicing-in an extra piece) and joined back together - you might find this approach useful, too, depending on where you're installing your LED.

. . . then fix it in position with two bolts.

Drill a hole through for the pin switch plunger, and install it in the hole . . .

. . . then drill another hole for the switch mounting screw, and secure it in place. It's advisable to protect your boot this way, too – but at least the boot might be protected by the alarm's voltage-drop feature (if you've got a boot light) or by the ultrasonics.

28 You must protect your bonnet with a "pin switch." If a thief gets your bonnet open unhindered, he can then attack your alarm siren and any associated wiring. Game over. Install your pin switch close to the battery, to protect the battery connections. First, make a rough platform to mount your pin switch on, then hold a pen or scriber vertically on it and have an assistant slowly close the hood. Mark where the pin switch needs to be, to work, bearing in mind the "contours" of the bonnet.

29 Your finished platform for the pin switch must be made of something pretty tough (metal seems obvious), otherwise it'll bend when the hood's shut. We just happened to have a nice thick piece of aluminum lying around, begging to be trimmed to size.

30 Drilling holes in your wing isn't usually a good idea. Here, it's essential. Drill through the flange at the top of the inner wing, and through your plate . . .

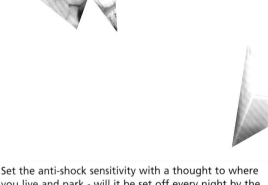

34 The only things left to do now are to connect the wiring from your alarm, and then to test the switch operation. The switch should be set very sensitive – the alarm should go off, the minute the bonnet latch is pulled. The switch plunger is usually made of plastic and can be trimmed with a knife if necessary. If you need to lengthen the plunger, fit a self-tapping screw into the top.

35 Now we're nearly there. Connect up the wiring plugs to the alarm/siren, and test it according to its instructions. Most require you to program the remotes before they'll work. Test all the alarm features in turn, remembering to allow enough time for the alarm to arm itself (usually about 30 seconds).

36 Set the anti-shock sensitivity with a thought to where you live and park - will it be set off every night by the neighbour's cat, or by kids playing football? When you're happy all is well, go around and tidy up the wiring with tape and cable-ties. There's a bit of a dilemma on the alarm fuses - if, like ours, yours are right next to the alarm module, do you tape them up, so a thief can't simply rip them out? Ah, but if you've buried them too well, you won't be able to install a new one so easily if it blows.

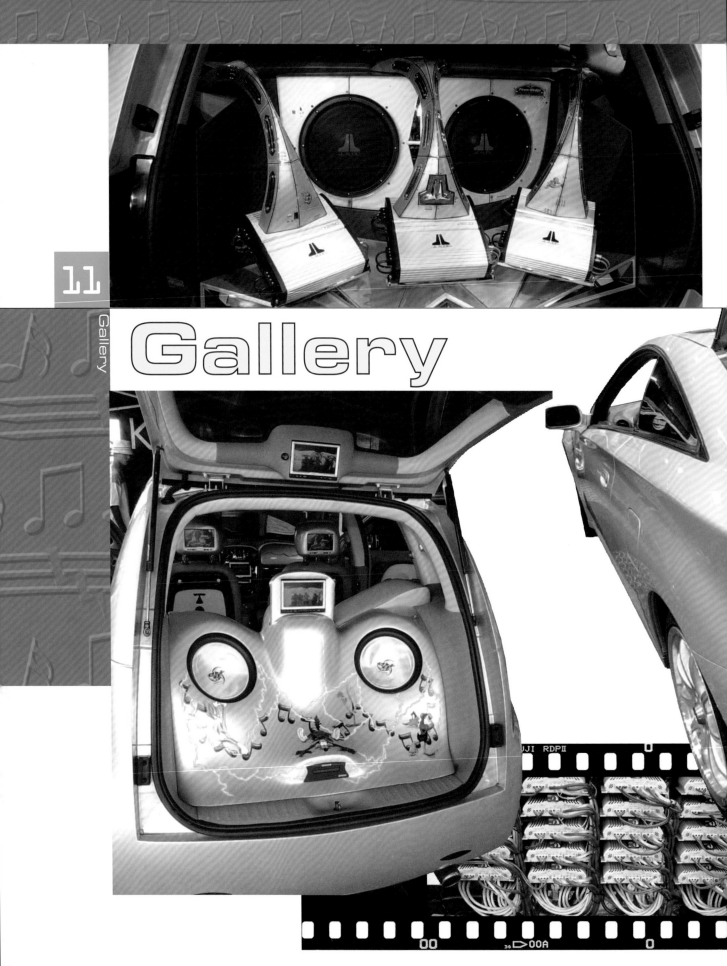

Gallery

WWW.CCGRAPHICSTUDIOS.COM

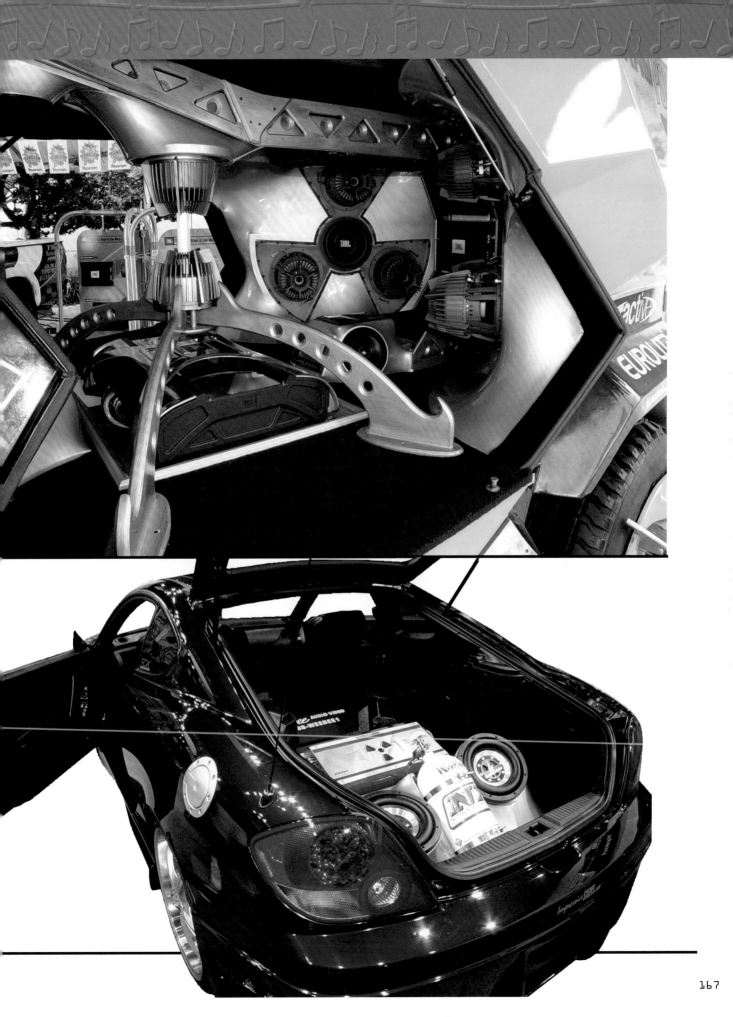

Photos by Paul Veldboom
(MEIsearch.com)

Glossary of terms

A

AC (Alternating Current) - Energy that alternates back and forth at a certain frequency. The frequency is measured in hertz. In automobiles, AC is produced by the alternator and then rectified to DC.

Acoustical energy - Energy consisting of fluctuating waves of pressure called sound waves.

Acoustics - A science dealing with the production, effects, and transmission of sound waves through various mediums.

Active arming - A method for arming a security system that requires some action by the driver/operator. This action could include pressing a button on a remote transmitter or entering a code on a keypad.

Aerial - see *Antenna*

Air horns - A type of horn that uses compressed air instead of an electric diaphragm or voice coil to produce sound. These horns are usually driven by an electric air pump that receives its trigger from a host security system.

Alarm reset - The property of an alarm system that resets the alarm to an alarmed state after a pre-determined period of time.

Alarm re-triggering - A condition that occurs in a security system that has been triggered. Instead of sounding the siren for its designated time interval, it is re-triggered and made to sound again.

Alternator - A mechanically driven automotive device that generates DC power; it is the primary source of vehicle power.

Alternator whine - A siren-like whining that occurs when an engine's RPMs increase. The noise is usually the result of a voltage differential created by more than one ground path or a poor ground path.

Ambience synthesiser - A unit that produces an artificial ambience pattern; one that is used to create the impression of the listener and/or performer being in a particular performance space.

Ammeter - An instrument used for measuring the amount of current flowing in a circuit.

Amperage - A unit of electrical current; the force through which the energy is pushed through a conductor. Measured in amps; Ohm's Law symbol is I.

Ampere - The unit of measurement used to determine the quantity of electricity flowing through a circuit. One ampere flows through a 1 Ohm resistance when a potential 1 Volt is applied.

Amplification - An increase in signal level, amplitude or magnitude.

Amplitude - The measure of how powerful sound waves are in terms of pressure.

Amplitude Modulation (AM) - A method of modulation in which the amplitude of the carrier voltage is varied in proportion to the changing frequency value of an applied (audio) voltage (see also *Frequency Modulation*).

Analog or Analogue - An electrical signal in which the frequency and level vary continuously in direct relationship to the original acoustical sound waves. Analog may also refer to a control or circuit which continuously changes the level of a signal in a direct relationship to the control setting.

Analog switch - A hardware-oriented switch that only passes signals that are faithful analogs of transducer parameters.

Anode - The electrically positive pole of an electronic device such as a semiconductor. A diode, for instance, has a positive and a negative pole; these are know as the anode and the cathode.

Antenna - A mechanical device, such as a rod or wire, that picks up a received signal or radiates a transmitted signal.

B

Arm - The term used to describe the act of causing a security system to reach a state in which it will protect the vehicle.

Arming delay - A term used to describe the elapsed time between the moment a security system is first told to arm and the moment it is actually armed. This normally applies only to systems that are passively armed, but it can apply to actively armed systems as well.

Audio frequency spectrum - The band of frequencies extending roughly from 20 Hz to 20 kHz.

Audio signal - An electrical representation of a sound wave in the form of alternating current (AC) or voltage.

Auto reset - The ability of a security system to automatically reset itself after being triggered.

Back-up battery - A separate battery added to the security system as an alternate power supply to serve as a backup in case the vehicle's main battery is disabled by a thief. Back-up batteries are typically the lead-acid gel cell type and are most effective when hidden from detection.

Ballast wire - The name given to a special resistance wire used between the ignition switch and the engine's high voltage coil. This wire is typically composed of a carbon compound instead of normal copper.

Bandpass filter - A device which incorporates both high-pass and low-pass filters in order to limit and attenuate both ends of the frequency range.

Bandwidth - Refers to the "space" in the frequency response of a device through which audio signals can pass (between lower and upper frequency limits, those points where the signal level has rolled off 3 dB).

Bass - The low audio frequency range, normally considered to be below 500 Hz.

Bass reflex - A vented enclosure that allows control of rear radiated sound waves.

Battery - A device that stores electrical energy. A battery makes direct current through a collection of cells.

Bias - An unbalanced sound level.

Boomy - Usually refers to excessive bass response, or a peak in the bass response of a recording, playback, or sound reinforcement system.

Bridging - Bridging combines two channels of an amplifier to turn them into a single channel, which increases the power output of that channel.

Brain - The common term used to refer to the main control unit of a security system (see also *Control unit*).

C

Capacitor - An electronic device that stores energy and releases it when needed. Also used to direct high-frequency energy to tweeters in the form of a passive crossover. Rated in Farads.

Cell - A single unit for producing DC electricity by electrochemical or biochemical action. A common vehicle battery is composed of a number of individual cells connected together. Each cell is typically rated at 2.11 volts; a common 12VDC automotive battery is composed of six separate two-volt cells.

Channel (security) - The term used to described the number of different functions possible for manipulating the buttons of a remote control transmitter.

Chassis - The metal frame of the vehicle.

Chirp - The term used to describe the brief sounding of a security system's siren designed to indicate the state of arm of the system.

Circuit - A closed path through which current flows from a power source, through various components, and back to the power source.

Circuit breaker - An electromechanical device designed to quickly break the electrical connection should a short circuit or overload occur. A circuit breaker is similar to a fuse, except it will rest itself or can be manually reset, and will again conduct electricity.

Clipping - Distortion that occurs when a power amplifier is overdriven. This can be seen visually on an oscilloscope, when the peaks of a waveform are flattened, or "clipped-off" at the signal's ceiling.

Closed circuit - A continuous unbroken circuit in which current can flow without interruption. Also known as a closed loop.

Closed loop - A feedback path in a self-regulating control system. Unlike a standard open state trigger that needs to have a connection established to serve as a trigger, a closed loop trigger will act to trigger a security system when its loop (connection) is broken.

Closure wire - The name given to describe a wire found on some vehicles that, when given a certain duration input, will cause the doors to lock and the windows/sunroof to close.

Code - The aspect of a security system that can be tailored by the manufacturer or the installer to personalise the particular system for a user or group of users. A remote security system that is coded will operate only with those transmitters that are coded to the same code.

Coaxial speaker - A coaxial speaker has a large cone for the low range and a smaller tweeter for the high spectrum. There is a crossover network that divides and routes the signal to the correct driver. Named for two speakers sharing a single axis.

Cone - The most common shape for the radiating surface of a loudspeaker. Often used to refer to the park of the speaker that actually moves the air.

Control unit - The central processor for a security system.

Constant output - An output of a security system that provides a constant or continuous output to drive a device. Often used for sirens and engine interrupts.

Control unit - The central processor for a security system (also see *Brain*).

Crossover - A device that separates the different frequency bands and redirects them to different components.

Crossover frequencies - The frequencies at which a passive or electronic crossover network divides the audio signals, which are then routed to the appropriate speakers.

Crossover network - A unit that divides the audio spectrum into two or more frequency bands.

Current - The rate of electrical or electron flow through a conductor between objects of opposite charge. Symbol I, measured in amperes or amps.

Current-fed aerial - An aerial in which the feeder or transmission line is attached to the source at a current loop.

Current sensing - A name given to a form of alarm system trigger that relies on sensing a change in the power supply of the vehicle. More accurately called voltage sensing, this feature is found on many inexpensive alarms.

D

Damping - The reduction of the magnitude of resonance by the use of some type of material. The damping material converts sound to energy, then disperses the energy by converting it to heat.

DAT - Digital Audio Tape

DC - Direct Current. A flow of electrons that travels only in one direction.

Decibel (dB) - The standard unit of measurement used to indicate the relative intensity of sound.

Dedicated fuse - A fuse designated to supply power and protection for one particular circuit only.

Destructive interference - A phenomenon that occurs when speakers are 180 degrees out of phase. For example, what one speakers is trying to produce, the other speaker is fighting to cancel. One speaker's wave is in the positive phase (compression), while the other speaker's wave is in the negative phase (rarefaction).

Diaphragm - A thin metal or dielectric disk used as the vibrating member in loudspeakers. Also known as a cone.

Diode - A two-electrode (two-terminal) device that allows a voltage/signal to pass through it in one direction only.

DIN - Deutscher Industrie Normen. German industrial standards that are used in many European countries. DIN size refers to the stereo size that fits most European cars.

Disarm - The opposite of arm, or the term used to describe the action of placing a security system in an inactive or standby mode.

Distortion - Sound that is modified or changed in some way. In a speaker, distortion is produced by several factors, many of which are related to poor construction. Voice coil rubbing (caused by being overdriven) is the most common cause of distortion.

DMM - Digital Multimeter. A digital meter that gives a precise reading of voltage, current, or ohms. This type of meter "samples" the input and feeds it to a digital readout.

Dolby System - A unique patented noise reduction system that electronically eliminates the irritating noise (tape hiss, circuit noise, etc.) without sacrificing the original tonal quality.

Dome light - The common term used to describe the overhead (or headliner) mounted interior courtesy light.

Door lock solenoid - The proper name for the electric bi-directional actuator used to provide powered control of vehicle door locks. Also called a *door lock actuator*.

Doppler sensor - Another name for a spatial type sensor, also commonly called a radar sensor.

Dress - The arrangement of signal leads and wiring for optimum circuit operation, cosmetic appeal, and protective routing.

Driver - Another term for a loudspeaker. Often used when the loudspeaker is coupled with a horn for acoustic coupling and controlled dispersion of sound.

DSP - Digital Signal Processing (or Processor). A type of processing accomplished by a micro-computer chip specifically designed for signal manipulation, or a component using such processing. The term is often misused as a synonym for ambience synthesiser; however DSP can do much more than sound field creation.

Duty cycle - An engineering term used to describe the actual time (or frequency) that a circuit or device operates. A pulsing alarm output that is on for seven-tenths of a second and off for three-tenths of a second would have a 70% duty cycle.

Dynamic range - The range difference between the quietest and the loudest passages of the musical selection or program signal being played.

E

Earth - The term given to anything that has an electrical potential of zero. Most modern vehicles are designed around a negative earth system, with the metal frame being the vehicle's earth.

Earth loop - The term given to the condition that occurs when a voltage potential exists between two separate earth points.

Efficiency - The measurement of a loudspeaker's ability to convert power to work. Formula: Efficiency = (power out/power in) x 100. Efficiency is always expressed as a percentage.

Electrolytic capacitor - A capacitor with a negative and a positive terminal that passes only alternating current. Electrolytics are available in polarised and non-polarised configurations. Non-polarised (NP) capacitors are useful as inexpensive crossovers, blocking low frequencies from passing through to mid- or high-frequency speakers. Polarised capacitors have specific positive and negative poles. This type of capacitor is useful for storing and releasing energy.

Emergency override - A button or switch, possibly separate or hidden from the commonly used controls of a security system, that is used specifically to override or disarm a security system in the event that the primary means is unavailable or disabled.

Engine immobiliser - A means, either electrical or mechanical, of preventing the vehicle's engine from either starting or running. The most common variety of engine immobiliser uses a simple automotive relay to inhibit either the starter or the ignition.

Entry delay - The time interval a security system waits before sounding the alarm after a vehicle's door has been opened.

Exit delay - The name given to the amount of time a security system waits once it's given a command to arm. Exit delays are usually found on non-remote security systems that rely on keypads or the ignition switch to arm. This delay gives the operator time to exit the vehicle before the system arms.

F

Fidelity - A term used to describe the accuracy of recording, reproduction, or general quality of audio processing.

Flashing lights - A term used to describe the interfacing of the vehicle's parking lights, courtesy light, emergency lights, etc., with a security system so that the lights flash by the system.

Flat response - An output signal in which fundamental frequencies and harmonics are in the same proportion as those of the input signal being amplified. A flat frequency response would exhibit relatively equal response to all fixed-point frequencies within a given spectrum.

FM - See *Frequency Modulation*.

Free air resonance - The frequency at which a speaker will naturally resonate.

Frequency - The term in physics that refers to a number of vibrations or cycles that occur within a given time.

Frequency counter - A device that assists in speaker parameter testing, as well as identifying the frequency of specific tones.

Frequency Modulation (FM) - A method of modulation in which the frequency of the carrier voltage is varied with frequency of the modulating voltage (see also *Amplitude Modulation*).

Frequency response - A term that describes the relationship between a device's input and output with regard to signal frequency and amplitude.

Fundamental frequency - The lowest frequency component of a harmonic series.

Fuse - A device designed to provide protection for a given circuit or device by physically opening the circuit. Fuses are rated by their amperage and are designed to blow or open when the current being drawn through it exceeds its design rating.

Fusible link - Designed to perform the same task as a fuse, but resembles a wire. Fusible links are commonly used in ignition switches and other high-current circuits.

G

Gain - Refers to the degree of signal amplification.

Generator - A rotating machine that produces DC electricity. Also an electronic device used for converting DC voltage into AC of a given frequency and wave shape.

Glass sensor - A device designed to detect the sound of breaking glass or metal-to-glass contact, thus triggering a security system. Also called sound sensors, glass-breaking sensors, or sound discriminators.

H

Harmonic - The overtones and undertones that define the acoustic difference between two sounds with the same fundamental frequency.

Harness - The universal name for a bundle or loom of wires that compose the wiring for a system.

Headroom - The difference between the highest level present in an audio signal and the maximum level an audio device can handle without noticeable distortion.

Hertz (Hz) - The unit of frequency within a specific period, such as alternating or pulsating current; 1 Hz = 1 cycle per second.

High frequency - Refers to radio frequencies in the 3-30 MHz band. In audio it usually refers to frequencies in the 5-10 kHz band.

High pass filter - A network of components which attenuate all frequencies below a predetermined frequency selected by the designer. Frequencies above cut-off are passed without any effect.

Horn (Audio) - Refers to a loading device when part of a bass enclosure, or a directional device when used with a high-frequency driver or compression driver.

Horn (Security) - Refers to the built-in factory horn in the vehicle. Factory horns can be of the diaphragm type, voice coil type, or air-pump driven type (air horn). All types of horns can be interfaced to a security system.

I

Ignition kill - A device designed to prevent the vehicle's ignition circuit from operating. An ignition kill device can work by either interrupting one or both of the primary wires leading to the ignition coil or by shorting out (grounding) the ignition coil's positive primary wire. Also called Ignition disable.

Ignition power - Refers to a source of power in the vehicle, controlled by the ignition switch, that has a +12VDC on it when the ignition key is not in the run and start positions.

Imaging - The width and definition of a soundstage. Instruments should appear to be coming from their correct positions, relative to recording.

Impact sensor - A sensor designated to detect various degrees of impact or vibration applied to the vehicle and then produce an output to trigger a security system.

Impedance (Audio) - A measurement of the resistance to the audio current by the voice coil of the speaker (see also *Nominal impedance*).

Impedance (Electrical) - The total opposition offered by a device or circuit to the flow of alternating current (AC).

Inductive coupling - Radiated noise that is transmitted through a magnetic field to surrounding lines.

Inductor - An electrical component in which impedance increases as the frequency of the AC decreases. Also known as coils that are used in passive crossovers.

Infinite baffle - A loudspeaker baffle of infinite space that has no openings for the passage of sound from the front to the back of the speaker.

Infrared sensor - A type of spatial sensor that uses infrared energy to detect an object (a hand, arm, or body) entering a protected area (see also *Spatial sensors*).

Input (Audio) - The high-level (speaker) or line level (RCA) signal connections that run into one component from another system component.

Input (Security) - Any wire on a security system designed to accept a signal from some outside source such as the vehicle's wiring. Door trigger, bonnet trigger, boot trigger and sensor trigger wires are all inputs.

Instant trigger - The term used to describe any trigger input on a security system that is designated to cause the system to respond instantly when triggered.

Integrity - The expected durability of a component or connection.

J

Jump - To provide a temporary circuit around a component or other circuit.

K

kHz - Abbreviation for kilohertz, or 1000 cycles per second.

L

Last door arming - A feature found on some security systems that enables the system to suspend itself from arming until the last door of the vehicle has been secured.

LCD - Liquid Crystal Display.

LED - Light Emitting Diode. A form of diode that sheds light. Used in many systems for indicator purposes.

Loudspeaker - An electro-acoustic transducer that converts electrical audio signals at its input to audible sound waves at its output.

Low frequency - Refers to radio frequencies within the 30-300 kHz band. In audio it usually refers to frequencies in the 40-160 Hz band.

Low pass filter - A network of components which attenuate all frequencies above a predetermined frequency selected by the designer. Frequencies below cut-off are passed without any effect.

M

Magnet - A device that can attract or repel pieces of iron or other magnetic material. Speaker magnets provide a stationary magnetic field so that when the coil produces magnetic energy, it is either repelled or attracted by the stationary magnet.

Memory - The word most commonly used to refer to a system's ability to retain specific information.

Microprocessor - A semiconductor that can be programmed to perform a variety of tasks in many different systems.

Midrange driver - A loudspeaker specifically designed to reproduce the frequency in the middle of the audible bandwidth. Most musical energy lies in the midband.

Milliamps - A unit of measurement of electrical current equal to 1/1000 th of an ampere. The milliampere is the most common unit used when measuring quiescent (minor) current drain.

Module - A term commonly used to describe a self-contained part of device that can perform a specific function.

Motion sensors - A sensor specifically designed to detect a gentle or sharp up-and-down or side-to-side motion of the vehicle.

Multimeter - A common term used to describe a Volt-Ohm-Meter, or VOM. A multimeter usually can measure volts, ohms and amperes or milliamperes.

N

Negative door switches - A common type of switch found on most modern vehicles which provides the trigger for the factory interior lights, key buzzer, factory alarm, etc.

Negative lead - The lead or line connected to the negative terminal of a current, voltage, or power source.

Noise floor - The noise power generated by an audio device in the absence of any input signal. It is generally measured in decibels.

Nominal impedance - The minimum impedance a loudspeaker presents to an amplifier, directly related to the power the speaker can extract from the amplifier.

Normally closed - Refers to the electrical state in which a switch may rest. Its contacts are held together or closed so that current is allowed to flow through its contacts.

Normally open - Refers to the electrical state in which a switch may rest. Its contacts are held apart or open so that no current flows through its contacts.

O

Octave - A musical interval between two tones formed with the ratio between the frequencies of the tone is 2:1.

Ohm - The unit of measurement for electrical resistance.

Ohm's Law - The statement of the relationship between current, voltage and resistance. Where I = Current, E = Voltage, and R = Resistance, I=E/R, E=IR, and R=E/I.

Open circuit - A circuit containing a switch, filament, voice coil, etc., which is not intact and current cannot flow through.

Oscillator - A device that produces an alternating current or pulsating current or voltage electronically.

Output (Audio) - The high-level (speaker) or line-level (RCA) signals sent from one system component to another, or the high-level signal from an amplifier to the system speakers.

Output (Security) - Any wire on a security system designed to produce a signal intended to be wired to some outside circuit or device. Siren wires, flashing light wires, and door looks are all outputs.

Override switch - A switch that provides a secondary means to disarm or override a security system in the event the primary means is unavailable (see also *Emergency override*).

P

Pager - A device designed to transmit a signal to the owner of a vehicle in order to alert him or her that the alarm has been triggered.

Pain generator(s) - A name given to a type of siren that is specifically designed to produce a sound of the proper volume and pitch so as to cause physical pain to a thief's ears.

Panic - The name given to the feature of a security system that provides the ability to the operator to cause the system's siren to sound at will. The panic feature is typically initiated either by pressing a button or buttons on the remote control transmitter by keypad command, by push button or by toggle switch.

Parallel wiring - A circuit in which two or more devices are connected to the same source of voltage, sharing a common positive and negative point, so that each device receives the full applied voltage.

Passive arming - The ability of some security systems to arm without requiring any direct action from the operator of the vehicle. Passive arming is usually accomplished when the operator exits the vehicle in the normal fashion (see also *Last door arming*).

Passive crossover - An electrical circuit consisting of capacitors, inductors, and resistors designed to separate an audio signal into specific speaker groups.

Peak - An emphasis over a frequency range not greater than one octave.

Period - The amount of time required for a single cycle of a sound wave.

Phase - The timing of a sound wave that is measured in degrees from 0 to 360.

Phase shift - Frequency interaction in the crossover region of passive crossovers that can cause some frequencies to be delayed with respect to other frequencies.

Piezo sensors - A type of shock or impact sensor that utilizes the properties of the piezo electric effect inherent in some materials. A piezo sensor typically uses a piezo electric element to sense impacts or vibrations applied to a vehicle.

Pinswitch - A simple, spring-loaded mechanical switch, used in many different vehicles, that's designed to turn on interior lights when doors are opened. Pinswitches are also used in the installation of most security systems in the bonnet or boot/hatch as a means of triggering the system if such points are opened.

Point of entry - The term used to describe the doors, bonnet, boot/hatch, windows, sunroof, or any other point through which a thief can gain entry into a vehicle.

Polarity - in electricity, refers to the condition of being either positive or negative.

Polarity reversal - A DPDT switch connected between a pair of DC input terminals so that the polarity of a pair of output terminals can be reversed or switched.

Positive lead - The lead or line connected to the positive terminal of a current, voltage or power source.

Power door locks - The feature where door locking and unlocking is performed by some mechanical means other than human power. Power door locks may be electric, vacuum, or a combination of the two.

Power line noise - A varying AC ripple that is found riding on a DC voltage. It is recognised by a whining that varied with engine speed.

Pre-amp - A circuit that takes a small signal and amplifies it sufficiently to be fed into the power amplifier for further amplification. A pre-amp includes all of the controls for regulating tone, volume and channel balance.

Proximity sensor - A common term for a spatial-type sensor that can be either the radar, ultrasonic, or infrared type (see also *Spatial sensor*).

Pulsed output - An output of a security system usually used to flash parking lights or honk horns; it is pulsed or turned on and off by the security system.

R

Radar sensor - A common name for a type of spatial sensor.

Range (Audio) - Usually described as frequency range, this is a system's frequency transmission limit, beyond which the frequency is attenuated below a specified tolerance. Also, the frequency band or bands within which a receiver or component is designed to operate.

Range (Security) - The term used to quantify the maximum operating distance that can exist between a vehicle and the remote control transmitter. Range is usually expressed in feet or yards.

Receiver - A device designed to receive a signal or command from a source such as a transmitter.

Relay - An electromagnet switch that allows small, relatively low-level signals to operate higher amperage devices. Also used when polarity reversal is necessary.

Remote - A common name for the remote control unit transmitter used with a remote security system.

Remote start - The feature where a security system or accessory module allows the vehicle operator to start the engine using a remote transmitter without actually being inside of the vehicle.

Reset - The ability of a security system to automatically stop sounding the siren and return to an armed state after being triggered, as long as no further trigger conditions are present.

Resistance - The electrical term used to describe the property that various materials possess to restrict or inhibit the flow of electricity. Electrical resistance is relatively low in most metals and relatively high in most nonmetallic substances. Electrical resistance is measured in ohms.

Resonance - The term used to describe the tendency of objects to vibrate at certain frequencies. This can be a useful or undesirable effect, as in planned enclosure or driver resonance, or as in unplanned enclosure resonance or wall resonance.

Re-triggering - See *Alarm re-triggering*.

RF - Radio Frequency. An AC frequency that is higher than the highest audio frequency.

Ripple - The deviation from a flat response in the passband.

Roll-off - relates to the attenuation of frequencies, above or below a given point, at a specific rate.

Roof-mounted aerial - A permanently-installed aerial located in the centre of the vehicle's roof.

S

Scanning - The popular term given to the way a thief breaks into a remote security system by quickly and sequentially transmitting all the possible security codes of a victim's security system.

Seat sensor - A pressure activated switch designed specifically for use in detecting any pressure applied to a vehicle's seat.

Sensitivity - The rating of a loudspeaker that indicates the level of sound intensity the speaker produces (in dB) at a distance of one metre when it receives one watt of input power.

Sensor - A device designed to detect or sense an intrusion or attack upon a vehicle by monitoring such things as motion, vibration, impact, sound, or the presence of a foreign mass.

Sensor bypass - The ability of a security system to automatically or manually delete or bypass the triggers from all or some of the sensors tied into the security system.

Shock sensor - A sensor that is specifically designed to detect a shock or impact applied to the vehicle.

Short circuit - The condition that occurs when a circuit path is created between the positive and negative poles of a battery, power supply or circuit. A short circuit will bypass any resistance in a circuit and cause it not to operate.

Signal-to-noise ratio - The s/n ratio indicates how much audio signal there is in relation to noise, or a specified noise floor.

Siren - Any kind of device, mechanical or electronic, that is designed to produce a loud warning sound when triggered by a security system.

Sound - A type of physical kinetic energy called acoustical energy (see also *Acoustical energy*).

Sound Pressure Level (SPL) - An acoustic measurement for the ratios of sound energy. Rated in decibels (SPL, dBA, SPL dBC).

Soundstage - see *Staging*.

Sound waves - Fluctuating waves of pressure that travel through a physical medium such as air. An acoustic wave consists of a travelling vibration of alternate compressions and rarefactions, whereby sound is transmitted through air or other media.

Spatial sensors - Devices specifically designed to detect intrusions into or around the vehicle by monitoring the space in and around the vehicle for intruders. These sensors work on a variety of different principles, including ultrasonics, radar, radio frequency, and infrared.

Spider - A flat, round, springy device that holds the vibrating cone of a dynamic loudspeaker. The spider is where the diaphragm meets the voice coil.

Staging - The accuracy with which an audio system conveys audible information about the size, shape and acoustical characteristics of the original recording space and the placement of the artists within it.

Starter disable - Any circuit or device used alone or in conjunction with a security system that is designed to prevent the vehicle's starter from operating.

Status - The state a system is in at any given time.

Subwoofer - A loudspeaker made specifically to reproduce frequencies below 125 Hz.

Switch - A switch is any form of mechanical, electronic, electromechanical, magnetic, or mercury device that either opens or closes a circuit.

Switch sensing - Refers to the inputs on a security system designed to detect a switch closure from such triggers as a door, bonnet, or boot/hatch pinswitches.

System reset - See *Reset* and *Alarm reset*.

T

Total Harmonic Distortion (THD) - Given as a percentage, a measurement of how much a device may distort a signal. Figures below 0.1% are considered to be inaudible.

Transceiver - A combination radio transmitter/receiver usually installed in a single housing and sharing some components.

Transducer - Any device that converts energy from one form to another, e.g., electrical to acoustic or vice versa. Loudspeakers and microphones are two types of transducers.

Transfer function - The change in the low end of a low frequency system brought on by loading the device into the cabin of a vehicle.

Transistor - An active (commonly three-terminal) solid-state device in which a large output current is obtained by small changed in the input current.

Transmitter - The name given to the hand-held remote control unit used by a vehicle operator to arm/disarm and perform accessory functions on a vehicle security system. More commonly called a remote.

Trigger - The common name for any time of stimulus that will cause a security system to produce an alarm. A trigger could come from a pinswitch, a sensor, or a direct command from a transmitter or accessory button.

Tweeter - A small loudspeaker or driver meant to reproduce high frequencies.

U

Ultrasonic sensor - A form of spatial sensor that is designed to detect an intrusion into a vehicle by monitoring the space within the vehicle with ultrasonic energy.

Unfused wire - Any section of wire between the power supply and a load that does not include the protection of a fuse or circuit breaker.

V

Valet - A word used to describe the state in which a security system may be placed in which it would be prevented from arming passively and/or actively.

Valet switch - The switch designed to provide the control to place the security system into or bring the system out of the valet state.

Voice coil - A coil of wire that takes in the electrical energy coming from the amplifier and converts it into acoustic energy or mechanical motion.

Volt - The term used to refer to the property of electrical pressure through a circuit.

Voltage - The electrical pressure produced to do work.

Voltage drop - The amount of energy consumed when a device has resistance in its circuit. The voltage (E) measured across a resistance (R) carrying a current (I). E=IR (see also *Volt*).

Voltage sensing - A name given to a form of alarm system trigger that relies on sensing a change in the voltage of the vehicle.

VOM - Volt-Ohm-Meter, sometimes called a Volt-Ohm-Multimeter. A multimeter that measures voltage, ohms, and milliamperes.

W

Watt - The basic practical unit of measure for electrical or acoustical power.

Wattage - Electrical power.

Wave - A single oscillation in matter (e.g., a sound wave). Waves move outward from a point of disturbance, propagate through a medium, and grow weaker as they travel farther. Wave motion is associated with mechanical vibration, sound, heat, light, etc.

Waveform - The shape of a wave.

Wavelength - The length of distance a single cycle or complete sound wave travels.

Window closure - The term used for the feature that causes the window(s) on a vehicle to close upon arming, or open and close as part of a convenience feature of a security system.

Woofer - A large dynamic loudspeaker that is well suited for reproducing bass frequencies.

X

Xmax - The distance a speaker cone can travel before the magnet loses control over the voice coil.

Z

Zero output - The absence of output signal or output power.

Zone - The specific area of the security system's coverage, or a term used to describe a specific trigger input.

Safety and tools

Safety

We all know that working on your car can be dangerous - and we're not talking about the danger of losing your street cred by fitting naff alloys or furry dice! Okay, so you'd be hard-pushed to injure yourself fitting some cool floor mats or a tax disc holder, but tackle more-serious mods, and you could be treading dangerous ground. Let's be honest - we have to put this safety section in to cover ourselves, but now it's in, it would be nice if you read it…

Burning/scalding

The only way you'll really burn yourself is if your car's just been running - avoid this, and you won't get burned. Easy, eh? Otherwise, you risk burns from any hot parts of the engine (and especially the exhaust - if you've got one, the cat runs very hot), or from spilling hot coolant if you undo the radiator hoses or filler cap, as you might when you're braiding hoses.

Fire

Sadly, there's several ways your car could catch fire, when you think about it. You've got a big tank full of fuel (and other flammable liquids about, like brake fluid), together with electrics - some of which run to very high voltages. If you smoke too, this could be even worse for your health than you thought.

a Liquid fuel is flammable. Fuel vapour can explode - don't smoke, or create any kind of spark, if there's fuel vapour (fuel smell) about.
b Letting fuel spill onto a hot engine is dangerous, but brake fluid spills go up even more readily. Respect is due with brake fluid, which also attacks paintwork and plastics - wash off with water.
c Fires can also be started by careless modding involving the electrical system. It's possible to overload (and overheat) existing wiring by tapping off too many times for new live feeds. Not insulating bare wires or connections can lead to short-circuits, and the sparks or overheated wiring which results can start a fire. Always investigate any newly-wired-in kit which stops working, or which keeps blowing fuses - those wires could already be smouldering…

Crushing

Having your car land on top of you is no laughing matter, and it's a nasty accident waiting to happen if you risk using dodgy old jacks, bricks, and other means of lifting/supporting your car. Please don't.

Your standard vehicle jack is for emergency roadside use only - a proper trolley jack and a set of axle stands won't break the overdraft, and might save broken bones. Don't buy a cheap trolley jack, and don't expect a well-used secondhand one to be perfect, either - when the hydraulic seals start to fail, a trolley jack will drop very fast; this is why you should always have decent stands in place under the car as well.

Steering, suspension & brakes

Screwing up any one of these on your car, through badly-fitted mods, could land you and others in hospital or worse. Nuff said? It's always worth getting a mate, or a friendly garage, to check over what you've just fitted (or even what you've just had fitted, in some cases - not all "pro" fitters are perfect!). Pay attention to tightening vital nuts and bolts properly - buy or borrow a torque wrench.

To be absolutely sure, take your newly-modded machine to a friendly MOT tester (if there is such a thing) - this man's your ultimate authority on safety, after all. Even if he's normally a pain once a year, he could save your life. Think it over.

Even properly-fitted mods can radically alter the car's handling - and not always for the better. Take a few days getting used to how the car feels before showing off.

Wheels

Don't take liberties fitting wheels. Make sure the wheels have the right stud/bolt hole pattern for your car, and that the wheel nuts/bolts are doing their job. Bolts which are too long might catch on your brakes (especially rear drums) - too short, and, well, the wheels are just waiting to fall off. Not nice. Also pay attention to the bolt heads or wheel nuts - some are supposed to have large tapered washers fitted, to locate properly in the wheel. If the nuts/bolts "pull through" the wheel when tightened, the wheel's gonna fall off, isn't it?

Asbestos

Only likely to be a major worry when working on, or near, your brakes. That black dust that gets all over your alloys comes from your brake pads, and it may contain asbestos. Breathing in asbestos dust can lead to a disease called asbestosis (inflammation of the lungs - very nasty indeed), so try not to inhale brake dust when you're changing your pads or discs.

Airbags

Unless you run into something at high speed, the only time an airbag will enter your life is when you change your steering wheel for something more sexy, and have to disable the airbag in the process. Pay attention to all the precautionary advice given in our text, and you'll have no problems.

One more thing - don't tap into the airbag wiring to run any extra electrical kit. Any mods to the airbag circuit could set it off unexpectedly.

Exhaust gases

Even on cars with cats, exhaust fumes are still potentially lethal. Don't work in an unventilated garage with the engine running. When fitting new exhaust bits, be sure that there's no gas leakage from the joints. When modifying in the tailgate area, note that exhaust gas can get sucked into the car through badly-fitting tailgate seals/joints (or even through your rear arches, if they've been trimmed so much there's holes into the car).

Tools

In writing this book, we've assumed you already have a selection of basic tools - screwdrivers, socket set, spanners, hammer, sharp knife, power drill. Any unusual extra tools you might need are mentioned in the relevant text. Torx and Allen screws are often found on trim panels, so a set of keys of each type is a wise purchase.

From a safety angle, always buy the best tools you can afford - or if you must use cheap ones, remember that they can break under stress or unusual usage (and we've all got the busted screwdrivers to prove it!).

DO Wear goggles when using power tools.

DO Keep loose clothing/long hair away from moving engine parts.

DO Take off watches and jewellery when working on electrics.

DO Keep the work area tidy - stops accidents and losing parts.

DON'T Rush a job, or take stupid short-cuts.

DON'T Use the wrong tools for the job, or ones which don't fit.

DON'T Let kids or pets play around your car when you're working.

DON'T Work entirely alone under a car that's been jacked up.

Source List

Accele Electronics Inc.
Car video systems and auto security systems.
www.accele.com

Alphasonik Inc.
High performance car audio products.
www.alphasonik.com

Alpine Electronics of America Inc.
Mobile multimedia and high performance car audio products.
www.alpine1.com

Audiobahn Inc.
High performance car audio products, speaker systems and accessories.
www.audiobahninc.com

Audiovox Electronics Corp.
Mobile multimedia and security products.
www.audiovox.com

Blaupunkt
Mobile multimedia and high performance car audio products.
www.blaupunktusa.com

CDT Audio Inc.
Automotive speaker systems.
www.cdtaudio.com

Cerwin-Vega
Automotive speaker systems.
www.cerwinvega.com

Clarion Corporation of America
Mobile multimedia and high performance car audio products.
www.clarion.com

DD Audio UK Ltd
High performance car and audio products.
www.ddaudio.co.uk

Dynamic Control
Acoustic control products (Dynamat).
www.dynamat.com

Eclipse by Fujitsu Ten
High performance car audio products.
www.eclipseb2b.com

Focal America
High performance car audio products, speaker systems and accessories.
www.focal-america.com

JBL
High performance car audio products, speaker systems and accessories.
www.jbl.com

JENSEN/Recoton Mobile Electronics
Mobile multimedia and high performance car audio products.
www.jensen.com/mobile

JL Audio Inc.
High performance car audio products, speaker systems and accessories.
www.jlaudio.com

Kenwood USA Corp.
High performance car audio products, speaker systems and accessories.
www.kenwoodusa.com

Kicker
High performance car audio products, speaker systems and accessories.
www.kicker.com

Magnum
General purpose and vehicle specific enclosures.
www.magnumrocks.com

MB Quart
Automotive speaker systems.
www.mbquart.com

Metra Electronics
Automotive stereo installation accessories.
www.metraonline.com

Mitek Corp.
High performance car audio products, speaker systems and accessories.
www.mitekcorp.com

Monster Cable Inc.
Automotive audio cables.
www.monstercable.com

MTX Audio
High performance car audio products, speaker systems and accessories.
www.mtx.com

Nakamichi/Nakusa Inc.
High performance car audio products.
www.nakamichi.com

Oz Audio
High performance car audio products, speaker systems and accessories.
www.ozaudio.com

Panasonic
High performance car audio products, speaker systems and accessories.
www.panasonic.com

Pioneer Electronics Inc.
High performance car audio products, speaker systems and accessories.
www.pioneerelectronics.com

Planet Audio
High performance car audio products, speaker systems and accessories.
www.planetaudio.com

Polk Audio
Automotive speaker systems
www.polkaudio.com

Rockford Fosgate
High performance car audio products, speaker systems and accessories.
www.rockfordfosgate.com

SAVV
Mobile multimedia and video.
www.savv.com

Scosche Industries Inc.
Automotive audio installation accessories, acoustic control products, cables and wires.
www.scosche.com

Sony Electronics Inc.
High performance car audio products, speaker systems and accessories.
www.sony.com /
www.sony.com/xplod

StreetWires
Automotive audio cables.
www.streetwires.com

US Amps Inc.
High performance car audio products.
www.usamps.com

Visonik
High performance car audio products, speaker systems and accessories.
www.visonikcaraudio.com

XM Satellite Radio
Digital quality, commercial-free radio.
www.xmradio.com

Xtant Technologies
High performance car audio products, speaker systems and accessories.
www.xtant.com

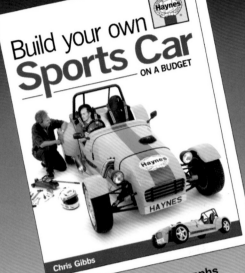

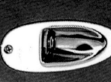